YOU GO GIRL!

Winning the Woman's Way

KIM DOREN
CHARLIE JONES

**Andrews McMeel
Publishing**

Kansas City

00 01 02 03 04 RDH 10 9 8 7 6 5 4 3

Library of Congress Cataloging-in-Publication Data
Doren, Kim.
    You go girl! : winning the woman's way / Kim Doren, Charlie
    Jones.
        p. cm.
    Includes index.
    ISBN 0-7407-0856-2 (hc.)
        1. Women athletes—United States. 2. Women athletes—United
        States—Biography. 3. Women athletes—United States—
        Interviews. I. Jones, Charlie, 1930- II. Title.

GV709.18.U6 D67 2000
790'.082'0973—dc21   00-21602

Book design by Holly Camerlinck

To the most important people in my life—my mom, my dad, and my sisters. Mom, you showed me what true compassion is all about; Dad, you taught me to strive for excellence and compete with integrity; Kathe, Julia, and Jennifer, you inspired me with your faith, your courage, and your creativity. Thank you for enriching my life. I love you.

KIM

The government (Social Security, IRS, Texas Highway Department) calls her Mary Virginia Calhoun. Her multitude of friends call her Virginia. I call her "Cissy." She's my sister, and she's the most wonderful, caring woman I have ever known. "Cissy," you're the greatest. This is for you.

CHARLIE

CONTENTS

FOREWORD

As the world is now turning, the future of sports in this country is squarely in the hands of the young female athletes. That is why *You Go Girl!* is such an important milestone. This gathering of some of the top women athletes in the world, sharing lessons they have learned from their personal experiences, is in fact a complete blueprint for success—success in sports and in life.

Kim and Charlie are the perfect pair to pull all this together. They get the conversation going, and then they get out of the way.

KRISTINE LILLY

INTRODUCTION

Sport is often said to be a metaphor for life. Through competition, we experience passion and pain, opportunities and obstacles, victory and defeat. The playing field provides an arena for self-discovery and personal growth. The lessons learned from sport are equally applicable to social relationships, school and business environments, marriage, and parenthood.

For years, women's participation in sports was relatively limited. However, the enactment of Title IX in 1972 helped shift cultural paradigms. Title IX is legislation that prohibits gender discrimination in federally funded schools and other institutions. Now more girls and women than ever before are taking part in organized programs. It used to be "She's pretty good for a girl!" but now it's "You go, girl!"

You Go Girl! was written as a catalyst to further motivate those who are already involved in sports, to inspire others to participate, and to share the knowledge and skills that sports generate. Athletics may be the most powerful resource parents can tap, in order to raise strong, healthy, confident young women.

However, the message of *You Go Girl!* goes beyond sports. The lessons in living shared here are applicable to all women, from the young to the more experienced, because even if they are not involved in playing sports, everyone plays the game of life.

The women you will meet in *You Go Girl!* are remarkable individuals, from those who have paved the way for this generation to others who are breaking new ground for future generations. They are powerful role models whose experiences provide encouragement and inspiration for all of us. We are grateful for the time and wisdom they have shared. From them you'll gain a greater understanding, not just about sports but about life. ■

ONE

FIND YOUR PASSION

"Each of us has a fire in our hearts for something. It's our goal in life to find it and to keep it lit."

MARY LOU RETTON,
*gymnastics star of the 1984
Los Angeles Olympics*

Julie
FOUDY

Julie made her first appearance with the U.S. national women's soccer team in 1988 at age sixteen. Since then she has become the team's de facto spokesperson. In addition, Julie is co-captain and designated comedian of the 1999 Women's World Cup champions. She is president-elect of the Women's Sports Foundation and will take office in 2001. Julie notes that the U.S. team feels pressure, but not from outside sources: "We're driven by ourselves."

My advice to girls is simple: Do something you love. It's got to be your passion. A lot of parents come up to me and say, "Please talk to my daughter about how many hours she needs to practice a day and what kind of weight training she needs to do," and these are seven-year-olds they're talking about.

The reason we've been successful on the U.S. national soccer team is we love to play, and as a result we get out there and practice and train a lot. We work hard and love to get better. So if soccer isn't something you really love to do, find something else. Maybe it's another sport. Maybe it's not even sports. But you've got to find what you're passionate about and then follow your passion. ∎

"We play because we love the game, we love each other, and we love to win."

MIA HAMM,
soccer star, member of the U.S. 1999 Women's World Cup championship team

"I love what I do. When I step on the track it is fun for me. I love getting to that finish line first. It's important that you love what you do, because if you don't there's no point going after it."

MARION JONES,
world's fastest woman sprinter

Gabrielle
REECE

Gabrielle (Gabby) was one of only three athletes named in **Women's Sports & Fitness** *magazine's "20 Most Influential Women in Sports" for 1999. Multi-talented, tall, and beautiful, she is a pro beach volleyball star, TV host, actress, author, designer, and model. Gabby emphasizes that her winning mentality is heavily connected to her passion for preparation. She loves to pursue her diverse interests.*

The most important thing is to enjoy yourself and experiment with as many different sports as possible. There's plenty of time to be dead serious about a specific sport when you get a little older. I think it's really important to have fun with it.

If you want to wear many different hats, you should go for it. Don't limit yourself by saying, "I'm only going to be in the National Honor Society and on the basketball team." If you also feel like being in the jazz club and being the homecoming queen, do that too.

Find something you love to do. I don't care what it is, and if it's not sports-related that's fine too. But it's really important to have something you are passionate about, something you feel good about, something you may even get good at. That is really what matters, because it will give you so much confidence.

Whether you're going on to get a scholarship and play college ball is not the point. The things you learn from being on a team—the discipline, relating to other women, working for a common goal, working with people you don't even agree with—these are all part of life. Use sports as a tool to sharpen your life skills. ■

"I get a mental high, a physical high and an emotional high because I love what I'm doing. I have a passion for it, and when all three come together in certain matches, there's no better feeling in life."

CHRIS EVERT,
winner of eighteen Grand Slam tennis titles

Sheila CORNELL-DOUTY

Sheila played first base for the U.S. women's softball team that won the gold medal in the 1996 Atlanta Olympic Games. She also won three gold medals in the Pan Am Games and two gold medals in the World Championships. Sheila was named ASA All-American thirteen times and was softball's Player of the Year in 1996.

The day of the Olympic gold medal final against China, Sheila admits she was nervous. However, she said, it was that good kind of nervousness you get before a big game. "The butterflies were there, but they were flying in formation."

You need to have dreams; everything starts with a dream. You have the ability to achieve anything you want as long as you are willing to work for it and make some sacrifices for it. You're always going to have people along the way who are willing to help you, whether it's coaches or parents or teachers.

I must warn you: Some adults will tell you that you can't do some things because you're too short, you're too tall, or you're not smart enough. But these are merely obstacles. Look at them as good obstacles—things to get over and go beyond. You shouldn't let anybody tell you what you can or cannot do. ■

"If a dream is worth anything, it must be worth failing for."

DAGNEY SCOTT,
former editor-in-chief of
Women's Sports & Fitness

"The most important thing is to love your sport. Never do it to please someone else—it has to be yours. That is all that will justify the hard work needed to achieve success. Compete against yourself, not others, for that is who is truly your best competition."

PEGGY FLEMING,
figure skating gold medalist,
1968 Winter Olympics

Claire
CARVER-
DIAS

As a young girl, Claire tried soccer, swimming, and diving and was successful at them. But as soon as she saw synchronized swimming, she knew it was for her. The use of music and the combination of artistic and athletic ability all were a great fit for her personality. Claire believes that if she's going to dedicate her time to something, she wants to enjoy it. Synchronized swimming was also a huge challenge. Her biggest motivational factor was that she wasn't really good at it right away, but now she's one of the best, as is her Canadian team. And the team is what matters to Claire.

I think a lot of our team commitment is a silent understanding that each one of us has poured our life into what we're doing. It's a precious thing. It's as if our commitment is really guarding that passion in everyone. We have a team creed we call "Our Sun." It says, "Our purpose is to be a team that is strong and true, a team of complete women who are centered by their physical, emotional, mental, and spiritual well-being. We choose to constantly pursue new heights in our quest for a gold medal performance in the 2000 Olympics and beyond. We believe in honesty, trust, and hard work. We know greatness will result from our passion."

This is the center of our team existence. Once you take the sun away, there's going to be no heat, no center to what we are doing, and we will fall off balance.

A lot of people say there's no "I" in team, but we all believe that is not true. At the Olympics we'll be nine individuals who'll bring our individual talents, our history, our past—our everything—to the competition. The way we love the sport is different for each of us, along with the reasons why we love it. We bring it all together. We're like little matches that together create a big fire. The fact that we share all this is our passion. ■

"Passion is timeless and priceless."

JILL LIEBER,
USA Today *sportswriter*

Michele
MITCHELL-ROCHA

Michele is one of those rare species, female head coach of a major college sport: diving at the University of Arizona. She won the Olympic silver medal in platform diving at both the 1984 Los Angeles Games and the 1988 Seoul Games. Like the 10-meter diving platform thirty-three feet above the water, Michele's expectations have always been high.

If you're female, there's an expectation that you have to be everything to everybody, and that's just not possible. I think today's generation of women feels too much stress because of that expectation.

When the floodgates opened for women to do it all, it was assumed they were *able* to do it all. There's a difference. To be able to do it all means to make good grades, have a meaningful job, be a loving wife and good mother, be active in the community, and be involved with sports. But there's just not enough time in the day for all those things. So what I stress to my girls is, first, enjoy the journey of being a woman and being good in sports, and, second, realize you can't do it all. Focus on the things you want to do most. I don't think a lot of mothers tell their daughters that anymore. It's okay to not do it all, and it's okay to not want to.

I think everybody has a gift. You should follow your gift. Some people are gifted as leaders, some as teachers. Others are gifted in science and they should explore that world, whether it's through the medical community, engineering, or research. Some people are talented musically, and they should pursue that gift. This is what I keep telling my students. A lot of the girls in college these days are trying to live up to too many expectations instead of trying to figure out what it is they want to do with their lives. ■

"Find something you really love that gets you going, so that every day you want to make yourself better. Once you find that, it's easy to stay motivated."

KERRI STRUG,

Olympic gold medalist in gymnastics, 1996

Liz
DOLAN

Liz is one of the most accomplished women executives in the country. She joined Nike just as it was about to explode on the international scene and rose to corporate vice president of global marketing, overseeing an annual budget of $400 million.

She then became president of Dolan St. Clair, sports marketing consultants, and the creator/producer/host of Satellite Sisters, an NPR radio show.

The most important thing for people to understand is what makes them happy. You can only be great at something that makes you happy. You'll never be great at something that doesn't, because you have to put so much passion into what you do in order to be great. You'll never do that if it really doesn't satisfy you every day.

One of the mistakes people make is not first just contemplating for a little while what it is they're really good at and what will make them happy, and then following that path. I never sat down and said, I want to be in a particular type of business, as much as I thought about what I enjoyed doing. The fact that I enjoyed doing it every day made me good enough at it to excel.

You're presented with choices as you go along, so that you actually do choose a path just by taking a certain job rather than letting an opportunity go by. But for me, there was never a master plan. I always took it day by day. I know that's really the opposite of what a lot of people say about how you should lead your life. It sounds very passive, but it's not. People say, "Oh, you should set these goals and you should go after them." I never set any goals except to be really good at everything I was doing. ∎

"If you don't have fun, you've already lost."

JENNY
CHUASIRIPORN,
*1998 finalist in the U.S. Women's Open
and the U.S. Women's Amateur Golf
Championships*

Kelly
WILLIAMS

Kelly is the U.S. national saber (fencing) champion and won the silver medal in the first women's saber World Championship. She also coached the men's saber squad at the University of North Carolina, where her first rule was that when the guys entered the gym for practice they had to check their egos at the door. Kelly's reason: "As long as your ego is attached to what you do in your sport, your focus is only on winning." She explains that if you're concerned about protecting your ego by winning all the time in practice, you can't improve because you play only to your strengths. You will only get better by concentrating on what you do poorly.

Kids start fencing because they love to fence; they love to play. Even before they understand what fencing is, little kids pick up sticks and play Zorro. There's a lot of history and a lot of fantasy involved in this sport. The one thing I want kids to remember is why they started fencing in the first place, which is the love of the sport, a love of play. If you get too caught up in winning or losing you stop having fun, and if you stop having fun, it's time to do something else.

I want the kids I work with to continue to grow and develop and to focus on getting better. I want them to have the discipline to work through the times when it's not fun and, at the same time, to remember the play involved and that it is a game. You grow and you learn and you get better and you get stronger, and you do all this through play. ∎

"I think sometimes we place so much emphasis on the importance of winning that we take the fun away. We try to let the kids realize that it's just a game, and yet they should play with a lot of enthusiasm, have fun, and do the best they can."

AMY RULEY,

North Dakota State women's basketball coach

DoDo CHENEY

By her eighties, DoDo had won 301 (and counting) national tennis championships, more than anyone else in history. She programmed her telephone answering machine to say: "Lob your message in. If it's not over my head, I'll return it with an overhead smash. Beep."

The very best win I ever had was the Australian Championship back in 1938. We got there by boat, and it took about three weeks. I had a marvelous time. I just loved it.

Yet I never took my tennis too seriously. In our day we just had so much fun with our tennis; we never trained very much. I remember one grass-court tournament I was playing in, on what was called the Eastern Circuit. I was called for my match and they couldn't find me. I was defaulted because I was out on the lake fishing with a couple of boys. That's how seriously I took my tennis back then. I just had fun all the time and managed to win a few here and there.

When I was twelve years old I was playing pretty good tennis and I was winning little trophies in the junior division, but if I played a twelve-year-old of today back in those days, she would have taken me in straight sets. They're so much better, faster, and stronger. Kids are now hitting those big top-spin forehands. They train awfully hard and I don't blame them, because there's so much money in it; it's their profession. However, I think the kids these days are under too much pressure—from their parents, from their coaches and from their agents—a lot of them get burned out early.

I just loved to play tennis. I wanted to play all the time. I never got tired of playing, and even in my eighties I'm still not tired of it. I'm still going strong. Maybe it's because I didn't take it too seriously and didn't practice too hard. I just love the game, I love to play, and I love the competition. Everything that's ever happened to me in my life that's good has been because of tennis. ∎

Marion
JONES

In 1998, Marion won an unprecedented 35 of 36 competitions in track and field (100-meter, 200-meter, 400-meter and long jump) and was the unanimous choice as **Track and Field News** *Athlete of the Year. A journalism/communications major while at the University of North Carolina, she was starting point guard on the Tar Heels basketball team that won the 1994 NCAA National Championship. Basketball may really be Marion's passion. She even has a tattoo of a basketball with wings and a lightning bolt on her right ankle, and she hasn't ruled out taking a shot at the WNBA.*

I was lucky as a child because I was involved in everything. While you're young, do as many sports as possible. Try anything you've ever dreamed of doing. Have a good time. Enjoy it as much as possible.

I was a tomboy growing up, so I used to play with my brother and his friends. There were no sports camps for girls. All the camps I participated in were male-dominated. The difference today is that all around I see girls' camps: in soccer, basketball, and softball. I think it's wonderful. It was a big shock for me when I went from racing in a boy's camp to running against girls. Girls act differently and speak differently, and it would have been nice to have been able to attend an all-girls camp, instead of being relegated to a room on the side with the only two other girls.

I also wish that when I was seven or eight there had been a woman athlete I could have talked to and learned from her experiences. That's why I get involved in a lot of clinics and camps, because if I can help one young person get started on something positive, that would be great.

As I got older I found out it's really important to love what you do, because if you don't there's no point in going after it. If you dedicate yourself to something, it's important to make sure and finish it off. I can't guarantee that if you step on the track you're going to be a Jackie Joyner-Kersee or an Evelyn Ashford, but I can guarantee that if you give it your all, people will respect you. ■

Evelyn ASHFORD

Evelyn is one of the greatest women sprinters in track and field history. She was a member of fifteen national teams and five Olympic teams and also competed in three World Cups and two World Championships: a very long career for a sprinter. In addition to winning four gold medals and a silver medal in the Olympics, Evelyn won nineteen national titles and was a two-time world record holder in the 100-meter. She said her defining moment came when she was six years old. Her teacher lined up the class for a race across the schoolyard. At the sound of "Go!" everyone started but Evelyn. When she realized what was happening she took off last but soon caught up and beat them all to the finish line.

I love to run. And I love the way it makes me feel when the race is right. I feel like I'm flying. It's effortless. I like the competitiveness and the one-on-one because if I win, I won. My teammates didn't help me. I did it. I think in track we're all individuals; we like feeling that it's our own effort. I just love the feeling of running. I love the challenge.

You have to have a passion for it. I don't think you can just say, I'm going to do this because I'm going to make a million dollars. You have to be passionate about it. As long as you have that passion, no matter what comes out of it things will be all right. You just have to love what you're doing. That's what I tell the young kids, because I loved what I was doing. I couldn't have done it if I didn't love it.

You even have to love training, because you are out there by yourself and you have to make yourself do the weights today, do the mileage today. You have to do all the little things that add up to that one fast ten-second race.

As far as athletics, I thought I had everything I needed. I didn't think anything was missing. I thought I could do whatever I tried to do. I would challenge myself to run a certain time in practice. It would be like a game. I approached it that way, as a game, to see if I could run a certain time. Then when I'd get to a meet I'd say, "Well, let's see if I can do it here." I constantly challenged myself. ∎

Andrea
JAEGER

Andrea became a professional tennis player when she was fourteen years, seven months old, and a month later she won her first pro tournament. She rose to be the number-two ranked woman player in the world as a teenager. However, a shoulder injury at the French Open, followed by an auto accident in which she fractured two vertebrae, cut short her tennis career at age nineteen.

That was when Andrea discovered her true passion. It evolved from visits she had made to children's hospitals while competing throughout the world. Andrea always dreamed

Kids don't come to the Silver Lining Ranch to get cured of cancer. They come to enjoy life. We show them something inside themselves that perhaps they never thought was there, so they can say, "I can do this. I can go to the top of Aspen Mountain. I can ride a horse on my own. I can lead a raft down a river." When you're lying in a hospital bed, these things become very important.

Actually, these kids are giving us a gift. They're giving us the appreciation of life. They don't want to be a statistic; they don't want to be a number. They have names, they have faces, and they have courage beyond what you could ever imagine.

of giving those kids a place they could call home, because they're in a hospital so much of the time. She co-founded the Kids Stuff Foundation and Silver Lining Ranch in Aspen, Colorado, to host youngsters with cancer and other life-threatening illnesses, to give them a childhood that illness was trying to steal. Through tremendous hard work and generous donations, Andrea's dream is now a reality.

I want to tell you about Rhea. Rhea was one of the teenagers in the first group we ever had at Silver Lining Ranch. She was from Chicago, and she made a big impression on the entire staff. There's a huge difference between young children and teenagers. Teenagers understand a lot more about boyfriends and girlfriends and marriage and careers and having kids. So, when they're diagnosed with cancer they think a lot more is being taken away from them than just their family.

Rhea came to Aspen wearing a wig. If you didn't work with kids with cancer you probably wouldn't have noticed it. She would tell us how frustrating it was that a lot of people didn't understand what she was experiencing. At her job they didn't even believe she was going through chemotherapy, and they didn't want to give her days off because she looked so normal. Her spirit was incredible. She was going through all this, fighting for her life, and yet she was enjoying every moment. She understood what it was like, not to know if you have tomorrow, so she was embracing today.

We were also dealing with younger children, and the differences were very obvious, because Rhea was going through the same thing yet she was helping the younger kids in the sessions. When it was time for Rhea to leave, she began explaining to us how she pushed grocery carts in and out of a grocery store during the midnight shift in Chicago, to earn money for gas to put in her mom's car to go take chemo. That's when we decided we were going to hire Rhea. We just didn't know what her job would be.

We called her as soon as she got home and said, "Look, we're going to be doing some different things. We can do a children's hospital newsletter that you can write and print and send out to hospitals for free. You can help us with different projects because you understand cancer; you're living with it. Why not use that in terms of helping other families?" Rhea was just screaming; she was so excited she couldn't believe it. So that's what we did in the four years we had Rhea.

She taped a video to show what happens with cancer over the course of time. She took us into the hospital, introduced her nurses, and talked to people in the hallways. She then videotaped herself while she taking her chemo. Each hour as the chemo was being administered you could see the changes. She started getting really sick. The color in her face would change. She'd start throwing up. She'd be crying. She threw off her wig. She was throwing up so much you could see the strain on her body. Eventually she just had to turn off the camera.

Every child touches you in a certain way, but because Rhea was in our first group she taught us so much. She would tell us how a lot of people don't even understand what it's like not to have hair, especially having no eyebrows. That looks different. It looks freakish. She would explain things that happened to her during chemotherapy so that someone who never had dealt with the disease in that capacity would understand what a person has to live through. Here was someone who knew what she was living with (we never say dying with) and helping us understand in greater detail so we could do more to help the other kids.

After four years of being part of Rhea's life, and Rhea being a part of the Foundation family, the cancer went into her bones. She'd gone through a remission and then she relapsed; there was nothing else the doctors could do. It's a silent policy that we don't go to funerals, because if we did we'd be going to a lot of them. (You can't just all of a sudden have the whole staff pack up and leave for a service.)

Rhea called and tried to make me promise I would come to her funeral. She had gotten the diagnosis this time, and it was only a matter of months. She didn't want to know the exact time, but her mom told me it wasn't months, it was days. So I flew to Chicago. Rhea lived in a trailer home that had holes in the ceiling, yet she had never ever complained. To see that, and to see the way she dealt with death as honorably as the way she dealt with life, was amazing. It was something you can't even imagine, and she was still so young, just going on twenty-one.

I stayed with her a couple of nights in her trailer. I slept on the couch. The cancer was eating away at her in drastic ways. I'd sit with her in the morning and talk with her and do the same in the afternoon. She'd have broken blood vessels in her eyes or in her legs. She'd be struggling to breathe when she talked. She couldn't walk well. She didn't eat. I'd come in her room and she'd say, "Hey, do you want something from my closet? You can have some of my clothes." I'd just sit there and think, How is she doing this? In a remarkable way, she was trying to give strength to all of us who cared for her.

One time she looked at me. We were just sitting and talking, and she said, "Everyone will forget me." This was in one of her darker moments. She didn't have very many dark ones; she was always making sure I was going to be okay. When she said that I looked at her—this was just a couple of days before she passed away—and I promised her that would never happen.

That's how Rhea's Tower came about at the ranch. Whenever Rhea came to Aspen, she loved to look in the sky for shooting stars. (In Chicago she couldn't see the stars because of the night lights.) She would look up in the sky for shooting stars, and we'd wander about saying, "Oh, did you see one? Did you see one?" So Rhea's Tower is the highest place on the ranch. It's the closest point to the stars. We named it so everyone would always remember her spirit and her love of life and her appreciation of the time we have here, because no one ever knows how long it will be. ■

"I don't think you choose this career. I think it chooses you."

ANDREA JAEGER

TWO

MAKE A COMMITMENT

"I do know that I train harder than anyone else in the world. Last year I was supposed to take a month off, and I took three days, because I was afraid somebody out there was training harder. That's the feeling I go through every day—Am I not doing what somebody else is doing? Is someone out there training harder than I am? I can't live with myself if someone is."

MARION JONES,
world-class sprinter and long jumper

Kerri STRUG

In the 1996 Atlanta Olympics gymnastics finals, Kerri missed her landing on her first vault and badly sprained her ankle. Then, despite excruciating pain, she leaped into history when she nailed her second vault and secured the gold medal for the United States. "It's weird," says Kerri. "I've done that vault millions of times, and I still can't figure out how I fell on the first one. I still don't know, and the doctors don't know, how I did the second one." Kerri later added, "My favorite was always the floor exercise. I think that's because it's the hardest to fall off of."

It's great to find your passion and follow your dreams, but it entails a lot more than saying, "I want to be in the Olympics." You're going to have to make a commitment to work really hard, to be motivated, and to be persistent. Remember, there are going to be a lot of bumps in the road. Sometimes you're not going to want to practice, and you're not going to get to be with your friends, but it's definitely worth it.

Don't just fit in with the crowd and be normal; try to be extraordinary. Competing in the Olympics is very important, and it's a great goal, but it's also crucial to set short-term goals. Not everyone can go to the Olympics, so you need to focus on other things. Most of all, make sure you really enjoy what you're doing.

Always set daily goals, because that's how you're going to get better in the gym. It can get a little monotonous when you train three times a day every day. If you don't have specific goals, you'll feel like it's just another day. So try playing mind games. Say, "Okay, I want to hit five vaults in a row instead of just four." You need little incentives for yourself to keep you going.

In each competition, have specific goals in addition to long-range goals. For instance, my goal may have been to make the national team that year. I think it's good to have different levels of ambitions, so you're not a complete failure if you don't attain them all. We all like a lot of self-satisfaction because it gives us more incentive to keep going. If you have a good perspective on your goals, you can feed off that. ∎

Lyn ST. JAMES

Lyn, the second woman and oldest rookie ever to qualify for the Indy 500, was named Rookie of the Year in 1992. Then she became the owner/driver of her own Indy racing team and, in addition, a television commentator, columnist, and corporate spokesperson. Lyn's motto: "Failure never occurs to me."

I had great advice from one of my early instructors, which was, "You're either on the gas or you're on the brakes. You are never coasting." There is a clear-cut commitment you have to make in auto racing: You have to commit to every corner entry, every apex, and every line. Every maneuver you make in that race car takes total commitment. Sometimes you're wrong, and that's when you spin or crash, but you can never hesitate; you can never be in no-man's-land.

It's an unbelievable experience to spend two or three hours driving a powerful piece of equipment where you are in a constant mode of total commitment. It's a wonderful exercise. I think that's part of what athletics is about. When I watch the NBA finals I feel that. You've got to shoot; sometimes you make the basket and sometimes you don't. I think all sports teach that, but somehow in our sport it's a little more intense. A great word for anybody who really wants to be a winner is the word *commitment.*

Commitment is what we experience the entire time we are in the car. That's what's awesome about it. There are no pauses; there are no breaks. The only time we have a chance for a little rest or a little reflection is when we're under the yellow flag or behind the pace car. The rest of the time it's total commitment. That's the way we should run our lives. It may be a little tough on those around us, but that's part of the price we pay to be at the level at which we perform. ■

"We are sometimes afraid to risk anything in life, or in sports. It's when you take the risk that you have the greatest success and sometimes the greatest failure. But a risk is a risk. That's what life is all about."

KELLY WILLIAMS,
national saber champion

Amy RULEY

Amy is head coach of women's basketball at North Dakota State, where she has won five NCAA Division II National Championships. Amy was college basketball's winningest coach of the 1990s. And she is justifiably proud of her 100-percent graduation rate of four-year players. Amy's coaching philosophy: "I'm not a yeller. My theory is that no one goes out there trying to screw up."

Everyone wants to win, but I think winners believe they *deserve* to win. They've made the commitment, they've followed the right path, and they've taken the right steps to be successful. That feeling comes from your off-season conditioning, your work in the summer, and your dedication and commitment in autumn practices. It comes from your work in the weight room, your understanding of the game, and your willingness to be a team player. You have to put the whole package together before you're going to be the person who comes away as a champion.

I think everyone believes she can win, but I think the winners really believe they *deserve* to win. They've paid the price, they've done all the right things, and they've put themselves in a position to have the opportunity to win. Then they get it done. ■

"The sickness I feel when we lose is a lot more intense than the exhilaration I feel in victory. However, I pay the price. A lot of people want to achieve success, but only a few are willing to pay the price."

VIVIAN STRINGER,
women's basketball coach at Rutgers

Claire
CARVER-
DIAS

Claire is Canada's top synchronized swimmer and the leader of their national team. She is a true team member, insisting that any publicity be centered around the team and not on any individual. In her solo performance, Claire portrays the strings, bow, and body of a violin in a gypsy-flavored routine.

My number-one thing I say every time I speak is that when you set goals, set goals for things you can control. It's fine to dream about being an Olympic champion, but when you set a goal it has to be something you can control. In my case, I can't control the marks from the judges, that's just part of my sport, but I can control how I train every day and I can control my performance. My job is to swim, not to judge. I can only control what I'm doing in the water. ■

"Goal-setting isn't restricted to being an athlete. In school and in life, setting goals is a good thing because it keeps me motivated to achieve them."

CLAIRE CARVER-DIAS

Amy
VAN
DYKEN

Amy became the first American woman to win four gold medals in a single Olympics when she accomplished that feat swimming in the 1996 Atlanta Games. Always a free spirit, Amy commented on the weight-training program for swimmers, "It's cool for a woman to be able to bench-press her husband." Diagnosed with asthma when she was only eighteen months old, Amy competes with a breath control that is only 65 percent of normal; she is not allowed to take medication that would make her 95 percent normal.

The medications that would help me are banned by the International Swimming Federation and by the Olympic Games. Without a doubt, I would get caught and I'm not willing to take that risk. However, I'm swimming against girls from other countries who are taking things to make them 150 percent of normal, and the chances of their getting caught are slimmer than my getting caught if I were to take asthma medication.

Those girls know they're doing something wrong. If I'm just using an inhaler to live, I don't see why I'm doing anything wrong. This is where the problem lies. I was in the hospital recently, and I was refusing medication that would improve my breathing. I was on the verge of choosing my sport over my life. My doctor told me, "You take this medication now, or I'm going to shove a breathing tube down your throat." I think the toughest thing to overcome is knowing that I have to choose my sport over my life. But I've made that commitment until the 2000 Olympics.

If I make the team, the Sydney Games will be it. If I don't make the team, my last race will be at the Olympic trials. I just can't mentally and physically put myself through what I put myself through every day beyond that. I'm going to be twenty-seven, and I push myself in workouts so hard that a lot of times I end up throwing up. I just can't see continuing that in my thirties. ■

> "I asked my coach if I get extra credit for throwing up during a workout. He said, 'No, no, no. You get extra credit if you make it to the rest room.'"

AMY VAN DYKEN

Sylvie
BERNIER

At age seventeen, Sylvie moved from Quebec to Montreal to work with a new diving coach, Donald Dion. This was probably the biggest decision she ever made in her life, because she was very close to her family and friends. Sylvie had just returned from the World Championships, where she placed seventh. But she wasn't satisfied. She truly had the feeling she could do more. It was either quit or make the

It was August 6, 1984. The Olympic springboard finals were scheduled for four in the afternoon. It was a beautiful day, very sunny, not a cloud in the sky. I remember talking with Liz Jack, my roommate, and she was telling me it was a beautiful day to win a medal. I said, "Wow, you know, you're right." I had a very light breakfast and I'd slept very well the night before and I was not nervous at all. I walked to the pool, had my first practice, and went back to my room. I remember that my mind was very clear. I had the feeling that I was ready to compete. I had had that feeling for many days before the competition, and I was anxious to get started. Finally, it was four in the afternoon. As always, I had my Walkman on my ears in between the dives. I was listening to "Flashdance," "Take your passion, make it happen." The music was very loud so I *move. Sylvie talked to her parents, and with their support she moved to a small apartment in Montreal where she cried a lot. Every day she asked herself, "Why am I doing this?" The answer was, Because she wanted to push herself to be the best in the world. And Sylvie became the best in the world; three years later she won the gold medal in springboard diving in the 1984 Los Angeles Olympics.*

couldn't hear the crowd. You have to remember we were in Los Angeles and the two Americans were among the favorites, especially Kelly McCormick, whose mother had won four Olympic gold medals.

In between dives I was listening to my music and trying to stay focused on my performance. I just did one dive at a time, and I had no idea I was winning. I was concentrating on what I had to do. I was only watching my scores, so I had no idea what the other divers were doing. After my final dive I remember waving to the crowd and feeling wow, it's over. I was very, very pleased. Then American diver Chris Seufert hugged me and said, "Way to go," and I said, "Way to go for what? What place am I?" She said, "Well, you may win."

That was the first I knew. Kelly still had her last dive. I was winning before that dive, but she still had the chance to overtake me. I remember standing on the pool deck and watching this one dive of the competition, which was Kelly's last dive. Then I saw the scoreboard and my name was in first place. It was an incredible feeling. I was so proud of the way I handled the entire competition. For me, it was just a matter of being happy with what I could do. It was not a matter of winning and beating Kelly and Chris and

Li Yihua and all the other competitors. I wanted to have the feeling that I had done everything I could do. That's exactly how I felt. I said, Well, if I feel that way and I win, great, I can't ask for more. ∎

"**Winning is not the end-all, be-all, but performing to the best of your ability is.**"

SYLVIE BERNIER

"**Those who truly have the spirit of champions are never wholly happy with an easy win. Half the satisfaction stems from knowing that it was the time and the effort you invested that led to your high achievement.**"

NICOLE HAISLETT,
Olympic swimming champion

"A true champion works hard and never loses sight of her dreams."

DOT RICHARDSON,
Olympic gold medalist in 1996,
U.S. national softball team

Carol
HEISS
JENKINS

Carol won the gold medal in figure skating at the 1960 Winter Olympics in Squaw Valley, California. She also captured four national championships and five world championships. Carol followed her athletic career by starring in the motion picture **Snow White and the Three Stooges** *and by becoming an outstanding figure-skating coach.*

Most of the kids who come to me have desire and ambition. They love to skate and they're young, mostly between six and twelve. I tell them, If you can't dream at your age, nobody can. They all want to be on the Olympic team or to be an Olympic champion, and why shouldn't they at that age? Basically, you've got kids who come in and are just beginning to skate and just starting to jump so I let them all have their dreams, their desires, and their ambitions.

They've got to have a strong commitment. You cannot believe how hard these kids work. They love what they're doing, but they have to be willing to sacrifice. Actually, they don't give up too much of their time or miss out on childhood as long as they enjoy what they're doing. It's like working. If you enjoy what you're doing, it doesn't feel like work, and you're not really missing anything, are you?

They also have to be honest with themselves, time after time, year after year. They have to be honest when they miss a jump to know they've missed it. They have to be honest in their love of the sport. They have to be honest in their goals, and most of all, they have to be honest with themselves. ■

"It's five-thirty, and it's snowy. It's Christmas Eve, but just think—nobody will be at the rink. I can train for five hours straight. And it will pay off someday."

CAROL HEISS JENKINS

"I focus on getting all the details organized—and there are plenty when preparing for an Ironman. I like to feel that by the time I start the race, everything I can control is taken care of, because there are so many things beyond my control. I also try to stay away from personalities I feel are draining."

PAULA NEWBY-FRASER,
winner of a record seven Ironman Triathlon World Championships

Claire
CARVER-
DIAS

Claire, a native of Missassuaga, Ontario, led the Canadian synchronized swimming team to a triple silver medal performance in 1999 at the German Open competition. Claire took second in the solo event. She teamed with Fanny Letourneau for another silver medal, this time in duet. Then, in the team event, the Canadians made it three silver medals in a row, as they finished second to the United States.

I believe that each human being has great potential, and I see that every day in each of my teammates. There's so much ability, talent, and drive inside them. Essentially, it's a trust thing. I believe in them and they believe in me and we are committed. Over the years we've shown our dedication to what we're doing, but even more, we're sharing a dream, and we trust each other with our dream.

The funny thing about teamwork is that when every person is equally important, if one person decides to be a slacker, or if one person totally messes up, it shakes up the whole team dynamic for a bit. When something like that arises, you either try to pull that person back into the strong core you have together or you lead by example, reminding her about the creed, reminding her about the dream. In a strong team, as soon as someone falls out of line, it's so apparent. Because it's like a culture; it's like she's breaking the law, the law of the team. But if her dream is real, she'll usually fall back in line. ■

"We're always yelling to each other, 'Let's go, guys! Let's push it!' And that extra push that you have from someone you respect and trust is so valuable."

CLAIRE CARVER-DIAS

Sheila
CORNELL-
DOUTY

Sheila was first baseman on the U.S. national team in Atlanta. After the team won the Olympic gold medal game against China, Sheila led them in a victory lap around the field, thanking all of the fans for the support they had given the team. Sheila said, "To be able to acknowledge them and to wave to them was great fun. Who knows? Maybe we started an Olympic softball tradition."

One of the most awesome things about sports, particularly team sports, is that everything you need to do to be successful on the playing field carries over directly into life. In a team sport you have to learn how to work together. You have to learn how to set goals and then work toward those goals in a productive way. You have to learn how to be responsible, not only for yourself but for your teammates. You need to be dependable—when you know what time practice is going to be, you're there for the entire time, not ditching out on it.

You learn not only to depend on others but also to be independent so you can support others. You learn a lot about loyalty and a ton about dedication. You learn how the results of hard work pay off in a game. I think every one of those things is something any employer would want of an employee. It makes you more successful in the workplace, because you've already experienced a lot of the same things in sports. ■

"Make it a point to be around those with positive energy—people who want what's best for you, people who understand your goals and priorities."

REBECCA LOBO,

Female Athlete of the Year,
and Female College Basketball Player
of the Year—all in 1995

Picabo
STREET

Picabo is truly one of America's most fun-loving, nonconformist athletes. Her name is an Indian word meaning "shining waters"; it's also the name of a town in Idaho. She was the first American to win the World Cup season title in downhill racing (1995 and 1996). In the 1998 Nagano Olympics, she captured the gold in the super-G slalom. With Picabo's enthusiasm it's easy to get caught up in her next commitment. She is recovering from surgery after her second disastrous knee injury and hopes to compete in 2002.

My commitment to the 2002 Winter Olympics in Salt Lake City is what is driving me to return to competition. That is really the big carrot. I can honestly say I would have already announced my retirement if Salt Lake City were not there. However, the fire still burns in me, and I look at the horizon and I can't turn away. I can't block it out. I can't deny it. It's there. It's my goal.

So I'm taking my time but I'm going back. I'm not guaranteeing anything whatsoever to myself—or to anyone else, for that matter. As far as results go, all I want to do is get back on the horse that bucked me off and have enough control to enjoy the ride again. Everything else will be a bonus.

I want a bronze medal in Salt Lake. This blows everyone's mind, I know. They say, "What? Why do you want to finish third?" It's simple. I already have a gold, a silver, and a bronze in the World Championships and a gold and silver in the Olympics. A bronze will complete my collection.

Rehab isn't easy. I'm like a caged animal going "Aaghh, let me out!" But if you want to be successful, you've got to make the commitment. ■

"I do not participate in any sport that has ambulances at the bottom of the hill."

ERMA BOMBECK,

on skiing, in her column

Debi
THOMAS

Debi's goal was to go to college and at the same time become the world champion in figure skating. She accomplished that as a premed student at Stanford University in 1986, when she became the first African American to win the gold medal in the World Championships. Her next goal was to attend medical school and also win the gold medal in the 1998 Calgary Olympics.

When I was five years old, my best friend's mother asked what I wanted to be when I grew up. "I want to be a doctor," I said. "You can't be a doctor because you're a girl; you have to be a nurse," she said. "My mommy said I can be whatever I want to be," I told her. Now, twenty-six years later, I'm finally going to be Dr. Thomas, making house calls.

I set those goals when I was very young, but not everybody does that. Only people who are really going to do something set goals for themselves. You also have to set little goals. It's fine to have the goal of being an Olympic champion, but there are a jillion steps you have to take before you get to that step. So you have to have the ability to set milestone goals along the way—goals that are realistic but are also a little bit above what people would expect. For instance, I said, "I'm going to go to college and become world champion at the same time," even though everybody said, "You can't do that, it's not possible; no one has done it since Tinley Albright." Well, it *is* possible. Granted, it's really, really hard, but you can do it.

I fell on my face a lot along the way. Luckily I don't have a fear of failure; that's often one of the things that holds people back. You really don't know what your true potential is until you've pushed yourself beyond your limits. You have to fail a couple of times to really find out how far you can go. If you make your goals too small, you may not realize you could do more.

My milestone goal was to be world champion. To get there I had to become national champion first, which I did the month before. But I also had some criteria. There was a certain way I wanted to do it. It was, Yes, I want to be the world champion, but I don't want to do it at the expense of my education. That was shocking to many; for most people I was competing with, their only goal was to win. I said, "World champion is nice but it's not going to be there for me when I'm fifty years old and can't skate anymore."

I made that decision because skating was something in which I only had a moderate amount of control. There were nine judges; I could skate great and they could still say, "We hated it." Whereas if I got my college degree and got into medical school, I had some control over my future. Granted, after I graduated I tried to get into orthopedics, which is pretty competitive, and I didn't get in the first time. But soon I'll be starting my first real job at thirty-one years of age. I'm going to be a surgical intern at the University of Arkansas Hospital in Little Rock.

I'm just so excited. Wow, I have a real job and I'm going to get a real paycheck, even though it's probably less than I make doing speaking engagements part-time. It's funny the things that will excite you. I just can't wait. I can't wait to be in the operating room when the surgeon says, "Dr. Thomas, you're going to do this appendectomy." I just can't wait. It's amazing the things that will really give you a high. ■

"Education prepares you for what's out there in the world. The world does not revolve around the sport of figure skating."

DEBI THOMAS

Marion JONES

Ever since she was a kid, Marion has been a versatile athlete. "My mom got me involved in a lot of things to keep me out of mischief," she says. Marion started track and field at age seven, and by fourteen, she was competing internationally. Marion became the first woman in the history of the World Championships to win back-to-back 100-meter titles.

There are a lot of people in my life who helped me get to this point—my coach, my husband—but once you get in the race it's all about you. I realized this in 1997. Trevor Graham, my coach, got me ready for the race. He prepared me mentally and physically, but when I stepped on the track and they introduced me, it was time to run the race all by myself. It was a shock. Trevor did all he could; he got me ready, but he couldn't hold my hand and run the race for me.

I train so hard to make sure failure doesn't happen. If I do everything I can, and run as fast as I possibly can, and still someone beats me, I don't think of that as failure. However, if I go out there and run a race that's not technically good, and my heart's not in it and I lose, that's a failure.

It's important when you train at such a high level as I do that you want to be the best. You should have the same mind-set for everything in life. That is what sets a champion apart from the rest of the world. Not only do I want to be the best on the track, I want to be the best if I'm playing a board game. Ever since I can remember I have been competitive. I think it's genetic. ■

"When I've done my best, I get goose bumps. Nothing is hard when you love what you do."

MARION JONES

"The difference between a good athlete and a top athlete is the top athlete will do the mundane things when nobody's looking."

SUSAN TRUE,
National Federation of High Schools Association

THREE

GO
FOR
IT

"In life, not just in sports, if you don't try, you cannot know what you can do."

MANON RHEAUME,
Canadian hockey star,
first woman to play in an NHL game

Joan
BENOIT
SAMUELSON

Joan started out as a skier, but when she broke her leg on the slopes she turned to distance running as a means of rehabilitation. By the time her leg was ready for the snow, she was hooked on running. Joan's first marathon was Boston in 1979. She got caught in traffic and had to run two miles before the race to get to the starting line. Joan went on that day to win the Boston Marathon, setting an American women's record with a time of 2:35:15. She won Boston again in 1983, but her shining moment was to come the next year in the Los Angeles Olympic Games.

I had just seventeen days to get ready for the Olympic Marathon Trials. At least the newspaper said seventeen. I think it was more like fourteen. I'd had knee problems starting on St. Patrick's Day, when I was on a long training run and couldn't really move the lateral joint. A shot of cortisone helped for a couple of days, but then my knee went out again and nothing helped after that. I had one more injection of cortisone followed by some anti-inflammatory medication, yet nothing seemed to help. I went to see Dr. Stan James and he operated on me, thinking I had no chance at the Marathon Trials because the event was so close. In my heart I knew when I went in for surgery that, if there was any way I could toe the starting line of the Trials, I'd be there. However, a few days before the surgery, which was an in-and-out procedure, I told Dr. James, "If you get in and it's a problem that's not going to allow me to run, go ahead and do whatever you need to do to fix it."

When I woke up in a hospital room with a big bandaged cast over my leg, I feared the very worst. Dr. James came to see me shortly after I woke up and said, "Do you wonder why you're here?" I was afraid to ask. He said, "Well, your reputation has preceded you. If I let you out today, you'd test this thing immediately." He was probably right.

I did stay off my leg for about three days before I started testing it. Nine days later I went on a 17-mile run with Lisa Martin, the Australian Olympian. I covered the distance and thought, If I can do that, I can run 26 miles. That run convinced me to go for it in the Olympic Trials.

I knew I could run a marathon, but I didn't think I could run fast enough. I'd taken practically two months off, having done very little running between the time my knee problems began and the date of the Trials. But I ran and I won.

A little over two months later, the day of the Olympic Marathon arrived in Los Angeles. It was slightly overcast, not my kind of day to run, humid and damp. I wished the air had been drier and the day a bit brighter, but the sun did break through the haze midway through the race. I don't remember much about the actual marathon except running down the Los Angeles freeway all by myself.

I didn't really expect there to be a lot of people watching. I thought, This is an early morning event. It is the first ever women's Olympic Marathon. It's the first event of the 1984 Games. There aren't going to be a lot of people who care about it. Was I ever wrong! The number of spectators who lined the course overwhelmed me.

Early on I was running in the lead pack but I was compromising my stride and stutter-stepping and not running efficiently. I just said to myself, "You know, you've got to do this on your own." That's what I tell everybody, "You can't depend on other people, you have to run your own race." So after about three miles I started to leave the pack. I didn't want to take the lead that early, but I told myself I would run my own race, and that's exactly what I did. ∎

"What's after the Olympic gold medal? Life."

JOAN BENOIT
SAMUELSON

"It's always better to focus on what to do now and not worry about what's going to happen later. If you're in the middle of a race, you shouldn't be thinking, I hope I don't die in the last mile. You worry about the last mile when you get to it. It's important to challenge yourself, to make goals and meet goals. But along the way, there's a process of learning and growing, and that's just as important as the end product."

NANCY RIEDEL,
*track and cross-country coach
at Mira Costa College*

Nancy LOPEZ

Nancy was the premier women's golfer of the 1970s and 1980s and one of the most popular players of all time. She grew up in New Mexico, where her father taught her to play golf at age eight. She went on to become a three-time LPGA Player of the Year and a member of the LPGA Hall of Fame. One of her many outstanding accomplishments was winning five tournaments in a row in her rookie year. She remembered how the streak ended. "I was standing over a putt thinking, Boy, I wish I had a Quarterpounder with cheese. That's when I knew my concentration was gone." Nancy went on to win a total of 47 LPGA tournaments and is still a fierce competitor on the LPGA tour.

The one tournament that stands out in my mind is the LPGA Championship the year I got my two-shot penalty for slow play. I fired a 63 on that day, but because of the two-shot penalty I was given a 65. That took away the greatest round of my whole career. I was furious at being penalized two shots for slow play when the other golfers in my threesome shot 77 and 78, and yet they were trying to tell me I was the slowest player. No way. When I went out the next day I was so focused I didn't hear anything anybody had to say to me, and I won the tournament. That win stands out in my mind as much as any, because I really made it happen. ■

"A winner will find a way to win. Winners take bad breaks and use them to drive themselves to be that much better. Quitters take bad breaks and use them as a reason to give up. It's all a matter of pride."

NANCY LOPEZ

Chris EVERT

Chris is one of the most beloved tennis players the United States has ever produced. She is the winner of eighteen Grand Slam tournaments: two Australian Opens, seven French Opens, three Wimbledon championships, and six U.S. Opens. Her international tennis ranking was never lower than number four in all nineteen years of her professional career. The mental part of the game was always Chris's strength. Good but not extraordinary as an athlete, Chris was exceptional mentally. She had the ability to concentrate 100 percent on every point, to go for it and not be distracted.

It's the mental part of the game that separates the winners from the losers. There are many great athletes and many great tennis players who are very, very close when it comes to the physical part of the game, but they're worlds apart when it comes to who plays the big points better, who concentrates better, and who's fearless.

Champions hate to lose more than they love to win. If you hate to lose, that's what keeps you going. That keeps you trying. If you want something badly enough in life, can't you make it happen? I mean, 80 percent of the time you can. I think you can make most of the things you want happen if you really want them badly enough.

It's the hunger, the desire. It's all the *Rocky* movies. I know so many gifted athletes who don't have the "eye of the tiger." I'm tempted to say most of it is bred or you're born with it. Perhaps a lot of it is need. Maybe those people are like me, maybe we have more insecurities, and we have more of a need. ■

"There were times when deep down inside I wanted to win so badly I could actually will it to happen."

CHRIS EVERT

Debi THOMAS

Debi graduated from Northwestern University Medical School and became a doctor, but her skating goal didn't work out as planned. At Calgary, Debi skated very well in the figures and in the short program and took the lead going into the long program. The gold medal was almost in her grasp.

I was so ready for that competition I didn't know what to do with myself. Typically, I'd spend hours and hours pacing back and forth in my room when I wasn't ready, but I didn't do that when I was ready. I just thought, I'm so ready. This time, I didn't do what I normally did in competition, which was to sit and concentrate on skating the best performance I could possibly skate.

I had drawn to skate last, which means you have to pace yourself as to when you start focusing about actually going out on the ice. It is also difficult because a lot of the adrenaline you had when you warmed up is gone by the time you've waited forty-five minutes. You're stiff. At that point I needed to be saying to myself, This is the Olympics. This is your only chance. You better go out there and give it everything you've got.

My coach tried to relax me by telling me that Elizabeth Manley and Katarina Witt hadn't skated well. But that was really irrelevant, because you can't go out and skate well if you're not thinking about what *you're* going to do. It doesn't matter what other skaters have done. You have to focus on *you*. I can't blame my coach, because I know he was just as nervous as I was. But I should have blocked it out.

Instead, I was standing there waiting for my music and I thought, You're not ready, I mean mentally, you're just not ready. Instead of the old me who typically would have said, Get your butt in gear right now, this is the Olympics, I said to myself, "Maybe my body will just automatically do it." I can't believe I actually said those words. I lost the Olympics right at that moment. I've never believed in my entire life that I could turn my body on automatic, so why, in the most important event of my entire skating career, would I say that?

My coach stressed repetition, repetition, repetition, but I was more of a psychological skater. We had different feelings, but in figure skating the only one who is going to make it happen is you. You're out there by yourself and your coach can't do anything for you from the sidelines. I knew better but I just panicked and said, "Maybe my body will just do it." What was I thinking? It was so unlike me.

I really wanted the Olympics to be the performance of my life. I didn't care what place I got, but I wanted it to be special. Then I two-footed my first big jump combination and it was all downhill from there. The only thing I could think of was, Well, so much for skating the program of my life. It's hard to come back from even the slightest mistake when your head isn't right, and my head wasn't right to start with.

I learned a lot that day. Unfortunately, you don't want to learn lessons at the Olympics. But I can remember skating later as a professional and making sure I did my visualization and did the things I normally do to psych myself up. I'm a strong advocate of, If you want it to happen, *you've* got to make it happen. And I didn't at the Olympics. ■

"If your head is not in the right place, you can't do it. It doesn't matter how much you train."

DEBI THOMAS

"My Olympic bronze medal is not one of the things I'm most proud of. If I had skated the program of my life and got a bronze medal, I would have been thrilled. But since I didn't come close to skating to my potential, it's very hard to swallow."

DEBI THOMAS

Evelyn ASHFORD

A world-class sprinter, Evelyn won five Olympic medals, four gold and one silver. "Now that I'm in my forties, I'm learning not to be as competitive, because it makes life easier," she says. For her first forty years, Evelyn was a competitor in everything she did, whether it was on the track or off. But she's tried to tone that down a little bit. Evelyn says it's really hard because her competitive juices get going on anything, even a trivia question.

My greatest race was the 100-meter dash in Zurich in 1984 after I had won the gold medal in that year's Los Angeles Olympics. Because the Eastern Bloc athletes had boycotted the 1984 Games, I felt I wasn't truly the best in the world. In fact, the media constantly pointed this out. However, the Weltklasse in Zurich is always one of the best track meets in the world, and 1984 was no exception. This was my chance to run against the world's best. All the athletes from the Eastern Bloc countries were there, including my East German rival Marlies Gohr.

In Zurich, the atmosphere is a little more intimate than in other outdoor stadiums. The spectators are closer to the track. You can feel their energy more. They are knowledgeable, and they are fans. They are absolutely into track and field. The atmosphere there in 1984 was especially electrifying because of the boycott. A lot of the East Europeans who had not gone to Los Angeles were competing in Zurich, which produced an Olympic feeling. It was phenomenal.

In Los Angeles, my feeling had been simply, Let me get this over with. I went through the boycott. I had a little injury. I was impatient. In Zurich, I was anxious. I can't describe it. I felt more competitive. I wanted to go for it, to prove that no matter who had been in the race in Los Angeles the results would have been the same. I was more nervous for this race than I had been at the Olympics, and winning an Olympic gold medal had always been my dream.

After the gun I was flying. I didn't touch the ground. I didn't feel the ground. The only way I can describe it is that I was flying. I felt weightless. It was the easiest race I've ever run. When it's right, you just don't feel it.

It was a perfect race. I ran a world record, 10.76, and I was vindicated—*yes!* ■

Inger MILLER

Inger is the daughter of Jamaican Olympic sprinter Lennox Miller, who won the silver medal in the 100-meter at the 1968 Mexico City Games, and the bronze medal in the same event at the 1972 Munich Games. Inger calls Lennox her role model. She remembers going to the track with him and running around thinking, "I want to be just like my dad." Inger saw the discipline he had. "Whatever he put his mind to, nothing could stop him," she says. I'm just like that. I'm hardheaded and stubborn. When I make a decision about something, I stick to it." She certainly did in 1999, capping a great season by winning the

I always had the knowledge and the faith within me that I could be the best. There were always naysayers, people who told me I should look into something else. But running is something I wanted to do; no one was going to tell me I couldn't.

My advice is this: Whatever it is you like to do—music, athletics, school, painting—your success comes down to self-discipline and willpower. If you want to do it, pursue it. Don't let anybody tell you *you can't,* because you can do whatever you set your mind to. If you want to be the president of the United States, you can be. Look at me—I've had people trying to stop me from doing so many things, but look where I am now.

The path I have walked has been long and arduous. I've been through injuries, car accidents, coaching changes, everything. It was rough. But having faith in *200-meter at the World Championships and receiving the prestigious Jesse Owens Award as the year's outstanding female track and field performer.* God and in his blessings gives you opportunities you need to take regardless of how they may turn out. Because in the end, everything will turn out okay. ∎

"I work hard all year long to do what I'm going to do for ten seconds. So I just do it."

INGER MILLER

Sondra VAN ERT

Sondra is the grande dame of snowboarding. In her thirties, did she have to undergo a character change to compete in a sport usually identified with the young and flamboyant? "I just forget my age." She laughs. "It sounds funny that you can mature and have more fun. But I've never had to grow up." Sondra is a former U.S. alpine ski racer at the World Cup level. While recovering from knee surgery in Sun Valley, she saw some kids having a good time on snowboards, decided to give it a try, and became a ten-time national snowboarding champion and an Olympian.

Competing in the 1998 Nagano Games was the neatest thing I've ever done. There's so much encompassing the Olympics, but to participate is what it means to me. It's something I've dreamt of doing since I was knee high. Just to be there with all the athletes, all the nations, the spectators, and the Japanese people who welcomed us was really special. I'll cherish forever the opportunity to have been a part of it.

I marched in the Opening Ceremony. The U.S. team was lined up, and we entered the stadium through one of the portals. As I came in I swung my head all the way around just to see all those people. I don't consider myself a showboat, but I threw my arms up because there will never be a stadium full of people for me again. It was pretty overwhelming.

In the giant slalom the conditions got the best of me. It had been snowing a lot and the course was challenging. It's a winter sport; that's the way things are. Sometimes it's icy, sometimes it's soft, and this time it was a combination of everything. I was going for it, and I spun out on a gate and went down. But I wasn't going to let it end that way, even though I knew I lost my chance for an Olympic medal. I got back up and finished my run, and the crowd greeted me like I was still a winner. It was amazing. My second run went a lot better. I wound up in twelfth place, ten seconds out, which is a mile in a snowboard race. That was it; some races go well and some don't. But this wasn't my Olympics. My Olympics was still to come.

We had been housed at the snowboard venue, about an hour and a half outside Nagano. After my race I went down to the real Olympic Village and hung out, just enjoying being an Olympian. I got to see my friend Picabo Street when she won her gold. I saw ski jumping; I saw the women's hockey team win their gold; I saw speed skating. I went to lots of events, and I walked all around the Village and all around town. I met athletes from all over the world. It was fantastic. It was special. *That* was my Olympics.

I don't let falling in the slalom make me a failure. How I judge success is all within myself. If I had gone down the course and been so nervous that I just tried not to make a mistake and then finished fifth or sixth, *that* would have felt like failure to me. But to go all out and want to win the race, that's part of my snowboarding. I finish half of them and I don't finish the other half, but I never give up. There's an occasion where a crash will leave me in a position where I cannot finish. But I finish half of them "queenly"; I'll put it that way. I call it "fighting for my right to party." I will always fight for my right to keep on going no matter what. ■

" 'Follow your dreams and chase after them with everything you have' is a message way beyond just kids. I think at my age of thirty-four it's a message for the masses. A lot of people want to attempt something. They'll think, I would love to, and maybe it's not even athletic, such as write a book, paint a picture, or play the piano. But then they think, I'm too old. You're never too old. It's really easy to do what you love to do."

SONDRA VAN ERT

"Most people's incredible feats are accomplished because they had the guts to try, not because of their skill and ability."

LOUISE COOPER-LOVELACE,
instructor at Eco-Challenge Adventure School and a breast cancer survivor

"If it's something you really want to do, something you love with all your heart, do it. You do things for you, not for someone else. Just because I'm female doesn't mean I'm limited."

STACEY SWAYZE,
thoroughbred jockey

Morjorie NEWLIN

When Morjorie won her first bodybuilding contest and the judge announced her age, the audience went wild. "I thought they were applauding because the old lady made it onto the stage," jokes Morjorie.

She was benchpressing 65 pounds when she was seventy-three years old, 85 pounds at seventy-four, and doing squats with a 100-pound barbell across her shoulders when she was seventy-five. Morjorie credits her mother for teaching her to set goals and achieve them.

When I was seventy-two years old I went looking in Philadelphia for a gym that would train me to use weights properly, and I found Bob Rivers. I told him I wanted to use weights and I wanted somebody to train me. He said he would. Had he looked at the record I filled out to see how old I was? I asked him if he minded my age and he said no. So we started working. He worked out with me and he started telling me about a show he was going to have in a few months. I thought he meant he was going to open the gym and show people in the neighborhood what was inside. He kept talking, but I didn't pay much attention.

I started in November 1991, but a month later my appendix ruptured, so I didn't really get started until February

1992, and this show of his was going to be in May. He said we had three months to get ready. I realized just before the show that it was not what I had thought it was. I knew nothing about bodybuilding, but evidently there was something he saw so he put me in the show. Of course, I had to ask questions all along the way such as "What do I do? What do I have to wear?" When he told me about the bikini, I thought, Well, I wear a bikini on the beach, but up there on stage by myself? But I promised Bob I'd do this, so I'll do it. I don't know what I'm doing, but I'll try. After I got up on the stage I said to myself, I'm not going to do this again. But then I won.

When the show was over, Bob said he had signed me up for a second show in another part of Philadelphia. So I did that one, and again the audience was very receptive. Evidently I have something that somebody thinks is all right, because I have now won about twenty-five trophies and medals. There have been times when I have won the overall and times when I've won first prize, but I don't mind if I come in fourth.

The nice thing is I've had so much support from women, and now a lot more of them are coming into the gym who never did before. I would recommend weight training for everybody, even young girls. I think it's good because it helps you to build a strong body. It really makes a difference. You don't have to go into that heavy business. Go over it with your doctor and see what restrictions you might have, but most doctors now agree it's all right. I know mine does. ■

"People say, 'When you get to be this age, you can't do that,' but that's not the way it is. I never considered my age when I went to the gym. I see some people terrified about getting older, but it's going to happen if you're still alive."

MORJORIE NEWLIN

Layne BEACHLEY

Layne is the first women's triple crown of surfing champion. She had to overcome a lot of problems along the way. Layne had chronic fatigue syndrome and has suffered with back problems, and in addition she has a demanding travel schedule. Layne will typically fly from South Africa on Sunday, arrive in California on Monday, and compete on Tuesday. But as she says, "These problems become the everyday norm you just work around. You don't harp on them. You just live with them."

My advice to young surfers is just keep trying. There are a lot of girls who are too intimidated to get out there and have a go. Fortunately, there's a lot more respect and a lot more encouragement for girls getting into surfing these days than there was when I was growing up.

When I first started surfing, if I went outside the boundaries at my local beach, I'd get told off and sent in. The guys would give me a hard time, and that really built my character. It taught me to give as good as I got and to come up with some really quick-witted responses. It really shocked them when I delivered some of them. That earned me a lot of respect in Hawaii, too. If I have an altercation with people,

I diffuse it really quickly by just telling them, "Listen, it's okay. You can't hit me, but it's okay."

For young girls trying to get into surfing, just know that if I can do it, you can too. Determination is the key. If you're determined and you commit yourself, you will have to work hard, but no matter how long it takes, in the end it's truly worth it. ■

"You've got to learn from every experience you have in life and keep it in the back of your mind. Don't dwell on it, but remember. You made it through then; you can make it through again."

LAYNE BEACHLEY

Nancy DITZ

Nancy was a late bloomer who went on to join the elite top fifteen all-time U.S. women marathoners. She was ranked number one in the United States in 1987 and 1988 and was a two-time winner of the Los Angeles Marathon. Nancy finished seventh in the 1987 World Championships in Rome, and seventeenth in the 1988 Seoul Olympics. With a smile, she shares her favorite story of her early running life. It happened during the first race she won. It was around Nancy's twenty-eighth birthday and her mom had given her a running outfit, a matching top and shorts.

I was one of four girls raised always to be a good sport, which is the way I'm raising my children. Because of this, I struggled my entire athletic career. I didn't start running until I was twenty-five. I played other sports and I always battled with the concept of how to remain a nice person and yet be a fierce competitor. I didn't reconcile this for eight years. It was not until the middle of a race in 1987 when I had an absolute epiphany. I was one of those people who would stand at the starting line, shaking hands with all the runners. My coach would say, "You can't shake hands with everyone at the starting line. You're giving away

Halfway through the race she passed her dad, who shouted, "Go, Nancy, go!" A little later she passed her mom, who shouted, "Honey, you look so cute in that outfit!"

energy. You should be focused." But it felt right to me to stand there and shake hands and wish everyone good luck.

In this particular race there was a teenage boy whose life's work, his father had decided, was to beat me, which was a little ridiculous because we weren't even in the same division. But his dad decided this kid should beat me, because then he would know he'd run a good race. I was running next to this teenager, and I was thirty-three.

He was trying hard but he was struggling, and I heard his father yell at him once for not passing me. So the maternal good-sport part of me kept thinking I should just let him beat me. I was still going to win my division, but at least he wouldn't get yelled at, and he would feel great because he beat me.

I wrestled with it. It was a six-mile race, and in miles one, two, and three he was a little bit behind me and I was letting him stay there and I wasn't pushing the pace. I could hear him gasping for air, trying to stay up with me, and I realized—something I have tried to share with as many women as possible—that the most nurturing thing I could do was to run my best race. By doing so, it would raise his level. All of a sudden I had no trouble with competition. I realized being the fastest, the best, or the strongest is the best thing you can do to further someone else's talent and ability. This came to me in the middle of the race, so I went ahead and kicked his butt.

I ran a great race and he wasn't that far behind me, so he probably ran a personal best. His father most likely yelled at him, but it really wasn't about him. It was about me—finally feeling comfortable being a competitor. ∎

"If you try hard and you have fun and you're a good sport, you're a success no matter what the score or where you finish. I think that's equally true at the Olympic level. You could be perfectly prepared. You could do absolutely everything right. You could run the best race of your life—and other people could beat you. That doesn't mean you are not a success."

NANCY DITZ

"Success is aiming for the stars, because if you fall short, you're going to land on the moon, and there are not too many people on the moon, now, are there?"

AMY VAN DYKEN,
swimmer and first U.S. woman to win
four gold medals in a single Olympics

FOUR

SHE GOT NEXT

"I think, as far as women in sports, we still have a long way to go. It's not about sport, it's about how to compete in our society. It's not being left out of the sandbox. We all have to play together and respect each other, and the sooner we learn to, the less discrimination there'll be."

DONNA DE VARONA,

winner of two Olympic gold medals in swimming, first female sportscaster on network television, co-founder of the Women's Sports Foundation

Nancy LIEBERMAN-CLINE

Known as "Lady Magic," Nancy is one of the most famous female basketball players in U.S. history. During her college career she led Old Dominion to national championships in 1979 and 1980. And both years, Nancy won a clean sweep of the Wade Trophies, Broderick Awards, and Broderick Cups. She got a lot of publicity and hype as a player, but she says, "In reality I was a blue-collar worker. I was a gym rat." Nancy was always the first one at practice, the first one in the weight room, and the hardest worker on the team. She adds, "Nobody saw that, they only saw the flash and dash." Nancy later became the head coach of the WNBA Detroit Shock.

I'm a fan of doing the right thing, so I'm not sitting here saying, "Women should have every job," because I don't think we *should* have every job. But I think we should have a fair *opportunity* for every job.

What's happened is that men who can't get men's jobs get the jobs coaching women. But women don't have equal opportunity to get a job on the men's side. That's what I mean when I say, "I wish some of those jobs had gone to women." I say it because either we get those jobs or we don't *have* a job. But, to be honest, I'm for the most qualified person. I just wish it happened on both sides. ∎

"I think men should be given the opportunity to coach women if they choose, just as women should be given the opportunity to coach men if they choose."

SHERYL SWOOPES,
*Olympic gold medalist and
WNBA Houston Comets star*

Michele
MITCHELL-
ROCHA

Michele is the University of Arizona diving coach, but she loves coaching fourteen-year-old kids. Their hormones are raging, they've discovered the opposite sex, and they've discovered independence. She tells them the truth—that it's really important to communicate with their parents. She reminds them that their mothers were once their age and faced the same dilemmas. "As a coach, it's a great position to be in because they'll actually believe you," she says.

I'm always amazed by how many men are coaching women. For instance, when you watch the Olympic Games and they show the U.S. coaches of women's sports, you see mostly men. Just about every sport I can think of, including figure skating, gymnastics, and swimming, are almost all coached by men. I'm one of only three women collegiate diving coaches in the entire country.

I see changes coming in college basketball. There are some great women coaches, such as Pat Summitt, but there aren't very many, and there are a lot of men coaching women's basketball. The same is true in women's track and field and women's volleyball. You can go right down the list, and there really are very few women coaching women.

I'm always perplexed as to why. Women can speak just like men; women can have the same experiences men do. A woman can win an Olympic medal as easily as a man can.

Interestingly, where the numbers are more even is at what I call the grass-roots level, not at the elite level. Yet when you look at countries like Canada, China, and Russia, you see a lot more women coaches than men. You have to wonder if in the U.S. equality has really taken hold. I don't think it's a glass ceiling. It's not that a woman can't get hired, especially at the collegiate level, because colleges have gender-equity issues they have to address.

However, there is still the expectation that if you are a woman you are the person who is going to rearrange your life for the kids, be the homemaker, cook, clean, and do the laundry, which leaves no time to coach. But somehow it's okay for a woman to be a coach at the grass-roots level, like after-school programs. I guess it's the maternal, nurturing thing a lot of these grass-roots coaches do. They work for Parks and Recreation or at the local gym, but somehow it's almost—I don't want to say odd, but when you see a woman coaching at the elite level—it's unusual. It *is* unusual, I'll tell you that. ■

"What my match with Bobby Riggs did was change the hearts and minds of people. You need a spark. You can legislate, but there are subtle ways around legislation. When you change the hearts and minds of people, and match legislation, then you've arrived."

BILLIE JEAN KING,
*on the importance of winning her 1973
tennis match against Bobby Riggs
(6–4, 6–3, 6–3)*

"I grew up always good at sports, but being a girl, I was never allowed to feel as good about it as the boys were. My toughness wasn't celebrated. But then I came to North Carolina, and it was okay to want to be the best. I loved that I didn't have to apologize for the fact that I got upset for missing a goal."

MIA HAMM,
*youngest woman ever on
U.S. national soccer team—
in 1987 at age fifteen*

"There is still a tremendous amount of ambivalence about girls being competitive in our society. But I think for girls to be really successful, in their personal lives, in a business or political context, or any other venue, they have to learn from boys and men about exercising their strength and power, and sports are a perfect vehicle for teaching that."

M. BURCH TRACY FORD,

Headmistress, Miss Porter's School

Andrea
JOYCE

Andrea is one of the best-known TV sports hosts in America. She has covered an impressive array of events, including NCAA men's basketball Final Four, U.S. Open tennis championships, CBS college football, and numerous sports specials. She co-hosted CBS's weekend daytime coverage of the 1992, 1994, and 1998 Winter Olympic Games, including the Opening Ceremonies.

I was the first woman sportscaster on television in Dallas when I started working weekends at WFAA-TV. There was some pressure, and I was a little nervous. I had been on the air for a couple of months when one morning I opened the *Dallas Morning News.* The local TV critic had written his column about how a certain sportswriter had been taping the weekend broadcasts, waiting for a certain female sportscaster to make a mistake, and isn't it a surprise that she hadn't?

This, of course, told me this guy wasn't very observant, because I had made plenty of mistakes. He just hadn't caught them. But I felt at the time, I'm going to be judged by a different standard here, and I better be very well prepared before I ever open my mouth. ∎

"Don't let them tell you no. If they say no, don't believe them. It's all about sticking it out. If you think you can do it, don't let anyone laugh at you. There shouldn't be some six-year-old girl thinking she can't be a sports announcer because 'women can't do that.' I was told I couldn't broadcast baseball because I didn't know what it was like to hit a home run over the left-field wall. I said, 'There are hundreds of thousands of obstetricians in this country who have never given birth. They are all men, and they'll never know what it's like, but they can deliver a baby.'"

SUZYN WALDMAN,
first woman to announce a nationally televised baseball game, later a broadcaster for the New York Yankees

Lesley
VISSER

Lesley is one of the nation's outstanding sportscasters, covering many premier sporting events around the world for ABC including serving as sideline reporter for ABC's **Monday Night Football.**

I was the first woman sportscaster to cover the NFL as a beat. I'll never forget my assignment to interview Terry Bradshaw after a Patriots–Steelers game. There were no provisions for equality then, so I was out in the parking lot with the wives and the families, waiting for him, when he finally came out.

I was there with my note pad and my pen, very eager and expectant. Finally Terry came over, but before I could ask my first question he took my note pad and pen, signed an autograph, handed it back, and walked away. ∎

"Yes, we [women] never played the game, but we can be great observers of the game, and interpreters, and we can relate it. I think that's just as important."

LESLEY VISSER

"I know, as a woman in the NBA, I'm going to be in for extra scrutiny and a lot of negative things will be said. I think I'm prepared for it, and I think I am doing the job for the right reason. I want to be the referee that I always wanted when I was playing, and I hope the players will forget my gender. My goal is to become invisible, which is what a good referee should be."

DEE KANTNER,
one of the first two women to officiate in the NBA regular season

Amy
TRASK

Amy is CEO of the Oakland Raiders and pro football's highest-ranking female executive. She holds a bachelor's degree in political science from the University of California at Berkeley and a juris doctorate from the University of Southern California. She represents the Silver and Black at National Football League owners' meetings and also provides legal counsel to the club. Amy says she is an outspoken person and "could not exist in an environment where I didn't voice my opinion."

I don't necessarily view myself as a woman in sports. I'm a Raider. I don't think I can comment on opportunities in general for women in sports. I think it goes back to holding on to your dreams. I'm fortunate enough to have found an organization where dreams really do come true. I abhor labels. I don't like labeling people. So I don't label myself as a woman in sports. I'm Amy Trask, and I'm a Raider.

My job is demanding, it's challenging, it's exhilarating. I have a passion for what I do. I think anytime someone is fortunate enough to feel passion for what they do, that person is very lucky.

I am my own harshest critic. There is nobody who has ever been as remotely critical of Amy Trask as I have been. I always meet a failure head on. I get angry with myself and resolve to never let it happen again.

I'm often asked, "You're the only woman who does what you do, how does it feel?" It doesn't feel because I don't give it any consideration. I don't consider that I'm a woman. It's not a factor. And if I don't want other people to think about the fact that I'm female, it would be wrong for me to do so. All I'm thinking about now is winning the Super Bowl. ■

"It's very important for the future of sports that we have more female leadership. Wherever I have been the first, I make certain I am not the last."

ANITA DEFRANTZ,

1976 Olympic bronze medalist in rowing, first American woman elected to the I.O.C. Executive Board, and head of the gender-equity committee

Cassie
CAMPBELL

Cassie started figure skating when she was five years old. When she wasn't skating, she was at the rink watching her brother play hockey. It took Cassie an entire year to convince her parents to let her play too. She finally got her opportunity when she was six, and she's been playing ever since. When Cassie was in her mid-teens, a lot of her friends were quitting hockey because it wasn't the "cool" thing to do. But since she really enjoyed the sport, Cassie continued to play. She was a collegiate star and a member of Team Canada, which won gold medals at both the 1994 and the 1997 Women's World Hockey Championships. Cassie says the key to her success is simple. "I have fun playing hockey."

I think young girls who want to pursue hockey really have to want to do it because they love it, because there are going to be a lot of obstacles. Especially today, because we're still not where we want to be. You must do it because you love it. You have to practice the basics over and over, like stick handling, puck handling, skating. Work hard, but more importantly have fun, and all that other stuff will fall into place.

It's important to have real respect for yourself. There are people who are going to try to pull you in different directions, so you have to have respect for the direction you want to go, and why you want to go there, and believe in that.

You'll have obstacles such as boyfriends saying, "Oh, you shouldn't be playing," and parents may not be very supportive because it's not a very "feminine" sport. I hate that. How many times have I heard that girls shouldn't play hockey? Or, "You'll never make money playing hockey, so why not try tennis or golf or some other sport that's a little more well known for girls to play professionally?" Those are the things you'll hear, the stereotypical things. A lot of parents are afraid to put their daughter in hockey because they're afraid she'll become a lesbian. Stupid social issues get in the way of what it's really all about.

I hate the words *feminine* and *masculine*, because who is the person who decides? Who decides who's more feminine than someone and who's more masculine? That's why I really don't like using those words, but it's the only way you can describe it. However, I think more girls are doing things like I'm doing, like playing hockey. Yet at the same time they are going out. I don't want to say I want all girls to dress in dresses, but you can do very normal girly things. It's important to be yourself and at the same time know you can go to the gym and sweat. That's okay. ■

Lisa RAINSBERGER
(formerly Weidenbach)

Lisa has won marathons all over the world: Boston, Chicago, Montreal, the Twin Cities, and Hokkaido, Japan. She was a three-sport All-American at Michigan in swimming, cross-country, and track. Lisa was the third daughter in a very competitive, goal-oriented, overachieving family. She had to do everything her older sisters did, and she had to do it better.

There is still a gender battle going on in track and field. Just look at the subtle differences, even the ad campaigns. I am so proud of the WNBA, because it takes women seriously. I know I can't change the world, but I can try to change things in my own way.

There was a race in Florida that always sent me an invitation. Every year I would call up and thank them and then ask if the prize money was equal for the men and the women. Every year they said it wasn't, and I'd say, "If I race the same race, the same distance, with the same effort as a man, but he gets double the amount of prize money I would receive, I can't come. I'm sorry but I can't send that message to the young girls who look to me as a role model. I'll be more than happy to participate when you have equal prize money." And then I'd always add, "I'm sure your sponsors take pride in being companies that have gender equity, and I'm sure if they knew the disparity between the men and the women's prize money, they wouldn't support that." The race director said, "You know, I never thought about it." And I said, "Well, maybe you should."

Finally, one year he called to ask me to race and said they had equal prize money. I felt I had made a little point; I had made a statement, and so I ran. I wanted to win, I'd given the poor guy such a hard time, but it was one of the hardest races I ever had. It went down to the last half mile, but I won. I feel proud I was able to get the race director to understand where I was coming from.

If we don't expect change overnight, and if we just stick to our beliefs, changes will be made. As soon as you start yelling and screaming, people stop listening. There's a subtle way of communicating, and I think that's why I don't feel like I've had any obstacles or roadblocks. I haven't allowed them. I have not put myself in a position to allow someone to take advantage of me because of my gender. ∎

"The one thing I wanted to do was show that it's okay to be competitive, aggressive, and ornery and still be feminine."

AMY VAN DYKEN,
Olympic gold medal swimmer

"I don't think being an athlete is unfeminine. I think of it as a kind of grace."

JACKIE JOYNER-KERSEE,

*winner of six Olympic gold medals
and holder of five world records
in track and field*

"When I was riding, do you know the body part I used the most? Arms? No. Legs? No. The brain, that's what. And my brain was as good as any man's."

PATTI BARTON,

*jockey who had won 1,202
thoroughbred races, a record for
a woman, when she retired in 1984*

Lyn
ST. JAMES

Lyn is an Indy race car driver and owner. She's on a mission to make her sport better by providing opportunities for up-and-coming drivers, both male and female. Lyn wants to change the rules just enough so that really talented people who aren't always traditionally accepted get a chance. She feels there's a lot of talent that goes by the wayside, and she would like to change that.

I think racing is a tremendous opportunity for young girls and women to be involved at any level, but there is a stereotype that women are more emotional, which is nonsense.

I deal with a 99 percent male crew, and I'm the quarterback when I drive the car. Think about it—the dynamics that are going on—obviously gender is an issue here. But when it comes to the bottom line, winning, auto racing is a genderless sport.

I remember telling some team owners, "Look, if I win it's going to be because you built a great car, not because I'm a great driver, because I'm just a girl." (You've got to figure some way to get them to think differently.) That's not what I really wanted to say, but meanwhile I'll try anything if it will help change their attitude. ■

"I don't like the oddity value of being the only woman in the field. I'd like to see ten of us racing. It's possible. It's not a matter of brute force in a race car. Success is based on the ability to withstand heat and maintain concentration. I don't think those are gender-based issues."

PATTY MOISE,
five-time NASCAR Winston Cup starter and competitor in the NASCAR Busch series

"It's not a man–woman deal, it's a racing deal. I don't think the car knows if it's a male or female driving."

JANET GUTHRIE,
first woman to qualify for the Indy 500

Liz DOLAN

Liz served as corporate vice president for Nike. She says that although there were people in business whom she admired, they were never people she wanted to be like. She has a need for balance. High-level corporate America was a great chapter in her life, she says, but it is not the book of her life. She thinks for a lot of business leaders, the big corporation is their whole book, but that doesn't interest her.

You can't reinvent the world as far as gender is concerned. So you have to work at putting yourself in an environment where you at least have a fighting chance and where you personally will be able to make a contribution.

That's one of the things I found at Nike. For me that environment placed a great value on individual excellence. People really had a chance to be the best, smartest employee they could be. There was a lot of leeway given to everyone, and even though it was very male-oriented in many ways, you personally were given the chance to do your best job, which enabled you to move forward.

You really can't fight the system. You can only do what you do well and put yourself in a position where other people will notice. ∎

"I think we can all see plenty of evidence out there that girls do not have the same opportunities to participate in sports as boys. That still needs to be corrected."

LIZ DOLAN

"Where I come from, girls are supposed to be china dolls and stay on shelves. Not me. I'm here to play, not to be displayed."

JENNIFER LLANERAS,
*fourteen-year-old artist
and softball shortstop at
LaGuardia High School in New York City*

"We're all in this together: women and men, girls and boys. It takes all of us to make the world."

BILLIE JEAN KING,
*winner of the Arthur Ashe Award
for Courage*

"There's not one definition of what is feminine, and what is beautiful, and what is athletic. And there will never be one answer to that question because everybody has their own opinion, their own perspective. So all I can do for my teammates and for myself is to get the message out that we are athletic and we are women and we are beautiful. See us for what we are and not for anything else."

BRANDI CHASTAIN,
scored the winning penalty kick that clinched the 1999 Women's World Cup soccer championship

"The world's not about boys anymore. There are women politicians, doctors, lawyers, and professional soccer players. It's girl power, baby."

MACKENZIE FENSKE,
twelve-year-old soccer player on the Medford (NJ) Strikers, attending the 1999 Women's World Cup games

Gabrielle
REECE

Gabby is a pro beach volleyball star, TV host, actress, author, designer, and model. She doesn't put success on a monetary or notoriety level; she thinks success is the great luxury of being able to do what you want to do. "At some point," she says, "success is your spirit as a person, trying to reach happiness or peace or joy." Gabby says that if you can get that figured out in your life, then you are a success.

I grew up in a household with a very athletic mother who was also incredibly feminine, so this combination just seemed par for the course. I was never taught you're either a volleyball player or you're a cheerleader. It was like, If you're moved to do either or both, go for it. One was not at the expense of the other.

My mom traveled in and out of being athletic and feminine. Even while she was being athletic she was still feminine. But also, I think it's just who you are. I'm someone who feels both of those things a lot. I feel really aggressive and athletic as often as I feel feminine and womanly and attractive. I know a lot of women I've played with and against who feel the same way.

Another factor is generational. I've had the liberty of not being confined to one thing but, in fact, being encouraged to go out and be all I'm motivated to be. But in my mom's generation it was sort of, "Listen, honey, you're either a jock or you're going to raise the kids and be a female, a woman."

We didn't have that and it's funny, too, because when I work with young girls now who are in the generation after me, the line is even more dissolved. It's not even a question for them. They have very strong opinions. The whole pursuit of athletics is not even a dilemma; they seem to embrace wanting to be girls. It's wider spread among the younger generation. It's also a social thing. And it's cultural, too. ∎

"There's a negative stigma that goes with being a female athlete, that you can't be feminine and still be an athlete. I don't think that's true. I think you can be a woman on or off the court. But you can also be a great competitor on or off the court. I don't think there's anything wrong with mixing the two."

REBECCA LOBO,
basketball star at the University of Connecticut, 1996 Olympic gold medalist, and WNBA player

FIVE

NEVER GIVE UP

"Success is never giving up, never letting yourself get lazy, and never allowing yourself to surrender."

KRISTINE LILLY,

U.S. soccer star,
key member of championship
Olympic and World Cup teams

Jean
DRISCOLL

Jean is a two-time Olympic silver medalist in the wheelchair 800-meters, in Barcelona in 1992 and Atlanta in 1996. She is also a seven-time wheelchair winner of the Boston Marathon and has an incredibly upbeat outlook on life. Jean was born with spina bifida, an opening in the spine. She walked with below-the-knee braces until she was fourteen and a freshman in high school. That year Jean was riding on a ten-speed bike and took a corner too sharply.

The thought that kept me going through the surgeries was, When I get out of this body cast I'm going to be able to walk, and maybe I'll be able to walk better. That was all in my mind. It wasn't something the doctors said, it was a hope I held on to. When they took off the body cast they sent me home to work on becoming flexible again, sitting up in bed, bending at the hips, bending at the knees. It was very painful.

About a week later I went back for some X rays and my doctor came in and said, "Jean, we're sorry. Your hip is dislocating again." I was crushed. I had hoped things would be different. Because of my disability, I walked laboriously and awkwardly. I was stared at a lot. Also, I didn't have normal control over going to the bathroom. There were plenty

The pedal dug into the cement and she slammed down, dislocating her hip. The doctors put a pin in her femur for traction, but that was just the beginning. Over the next year Jean had five major hip operations and spent the entire year in a body cast.

of situations that were humbling and embarrassing, no matter where I was or who I was with, which made me feel like I was at the very bottom of the totem pole.

I didn't have much self-esteem except for academics. I wasn't a straight-A student but I was low A or high B. I got better report cards than my brothers did. They were faster, more coordinated, but I was more intelligent, and there were bonus points to be earned from that. My sister was out of reach. She was beautiful, she was smart, she got straight A's without studying, and she was going to be the first female president of the United States. I couldn't touch her. We didn't get along, not at all.

Because none of the surgeries worked I had to start walking with crutches and, even worse, I got my first wheelchair. I was fifteen. I had the same ideas about a wheelchair that everybody has. I thought it was very limiting. I thought it was going to make me dependent. I thought opportunities in life were being stripped away from me. Before, I walked funny, but at least I could walk and do things, but now I was stuck in this wheelchair. I didn't know what I was going to do.

Everyone started telling me I'd better take all those secretarial-type courses, typing and stenography and such, because I was going to be a secretary. It's the only sit-down job there is. I kept thinking, My sister is going to be the first female president of the United States, but I am *not* going to be her secretary.

I was at a college-prep all-girls school and was not up to speed with my classmates when I returned. So, for my junior and senior years, I transferred to a public school, Custer High, where I could graduate on time. At Custer, I met another kid who used a wheelchair. His name was Jim and, like me, he also had been born with spina bifida. He asked me if I'd ever heard of wheelchair soccer. I said, "Wheelchair soccer? How do you play wheelchair soccer? You need your legs to play soccer." He said, "No, it's adapted." I hate that word *adapted,* and I thought, No way. It's going to be so stupid. I'm not going to hang out with those wheelchair people. I'm not one of those wheelchair people. They're weird. They're not normal. I don't want people to think the only boyfriends I can get are guys in wheelchairs, that my only friends are people in wheelchairs.

I resisted Jim's invitations to wheelchair soccer practice for the whole year, but he just wouldn't stop asking me. Finally, in May of my junior year, to get rid of this guy I told him I would go to a practice. I knew I was not going to like it, but at least I'd get this guy off my back.

His mom came and picked me up, and I went to the soccer practice. Wow! It was so competitive. Chairs were crashing and banging. Bodies were flying. This was *sports.* I'd always been team manager or scorekeeper or statistician; I couldn't ever get in the game. Now suddenly I had an opportunity to get down and dirty and mix it up with everybody.

The coaches didn't freak out when people fell over in their chairs. Sure, some needed help getting back up, but they got back up. A lot of time people get upset when they see somebody in a wheelchair falling over. But what does Michael Jordan do? What does anybody do? If you fall over in public, you look around, make sure nobody saw you, get back up, and keep going. That is what the coaches let us do.

For the first time I started to see a little differently, but it took a long time for me to get a proper handle on my disability and my body. After soccer there was wheelchair football and then ice hockey. It was so much fun. A whole new world opened up.

I tried almost every sport, and then I started college at the University at Wisconsin in Milwaukee. After three semesters I flunked out. My parents were going through a divorce. I still didn't like myself. I wasn't dealing with my disability very well. I felt I was a burden and a financial drain, and I kept having little medical problems that made me miss a week of school here, two weeks of school there. I hit rock bottom. School was the only thing that gave me my self-esteem. It was the only thing I felt I could control, and all of a sudden I had lost control there too.

I was suicidal for a short time. I was trying to figure out where I was going and who I was, but I was still involved in wheelchair sports programs and activities in Milwaukee. Brad Hedrick, who was the supervisor of the wheelchair sports program at the University of Illinois, saw me playing an exhibition game of wheelchair soccer and tried to recruit me. But I wasn't buying it right away. There's a huge rivalry between Wisconsin and Illinois, especially between Milwaukee and Chicago. It's huge. So I kept thinking, What does Illinois have to offer me? He was sending me letters, calling me regularly, and I was flattered by his persistence. I'd never had anybody show an interest in me like that, especially regarding sports. I started thinking, Maybe a change is what I need in my life, so I accepted his offer.

In August of 1987, I moved to Champaign, Illinois, and from the day I arrived on campus my life changed. I am such a different person now from the insecure, reactive (as opposed to proactive), frightened girl from Milwaukee. I didn't know how to set goals. I blamed my disability for everything. It was the reason why I didn't get the boyfriends I wanted, why I didn't get the baby-sitting jobs or any other things I wanted. It was my focus.

All of a sudden I came to Illinois and there were people using wheelchairs who were going for master's degrees and Ph.D.s. They were going to the Olympic Games. They were getting married. They were doing all these things that "normal" people do, and I had never felt "normal" in my entire life. Suddenly I realized being in a wheelchair couldn't be an excuse anymore. I promised myself when I came down here I wouldn't ever flunk out of school again. I just couldn't do it. I wanted to have the frame of mind and the confidence these other people had.

Those were my first goals, but I needed people in my life like Brad Hedrick and my racing coach, Marty Morse, who saw potential in me long before I ever saw potential in myself. All of a sudden the disability stopped being my focus and moved out and became a characteristic instead, like hair or eye color. I've gone to the Olympic Games and won two silver medals, I've won the Boston Marathon seven times, and I've won the Los Angeles Marathon. I've had amazing life experiences, which had nothing to do with my disability and everything to do with my ability.

The University of Illinois Liberal Arts and Sciences College honored me with its Alumni Achievement Award. My first reaction was, I don't deserve this. I'm too young, only thirty-one. People who get awards are fifty, sixty, seventy years old. They have a lifetime of huge things they've done. I received my achievement award along with a man who helped develop the MRI. How small does that make you feel? His contribution was so phenomenal and yet they were saying, "Jean, you have no idea what you have done. You deserve this." Brad Hedrick was one of the people who wrote a nomination letter for me. I went in and told him I didn't feel I deserved this, not yet anyway. And he said, "Well, then, spend the rest of your life earning it."

I love the platform I have now on which I get to speak and get to educate. I get to talk about being a 1996 Olympic silver medalist in the wheelchair 800-meters, being in Atlanta on my own home country turf, and accepting my silver medal. When the announcer introduced me as being an American, 86,000 people stood up in the stands and cheered wildly. I still get chills thinking about it. It was phenomenal. I've done things in my life that most people can only dream about doing, and my disability has nothing to do with it. I've persevered through many things, but if I'm inspirational, I want it to be in a motivational way. If I'm inspiring somebody, I hope I'm inspiring them to go out and *do* something.

In addition, I did find that sit-down job. I'm sitting in my racing chair. And just as important, my sister and I now have great respect for each other. ■

"My Olympic medals are covered with the fingerprints of fans I have shared them with. I love that."

JEAN DRISCOLL

"Ultimately, success is not measured by first-place prizes. It's measured by the road we have traveled, how you dealt with the challenges and the stumbling blocks you encountered along the way."

NICOLE HAISLETT,
winner of three Olympic gold medals in swimming

Kelly WILLIAMS

Kelly is the U.S. women's national saber champion. She does not have a fear of failure; she knows that it is only through failure that she becomes stronger. When she lost in the finals of the World Championships, she was challenged to look at why she lost, to make adjustments, and to train harder. As Kelly says, "If you haven't fallen, you're not learning."

Winning the Division I National Championship was my greatest victory. Going into the tournament I was number two in the national standings, and only the top-ranked fencer makes the world championship team. My chief competitor was Chris Becker from Oregon. She was ahead of me in the standings, but if I won this tournament I would finish the season number one.

I knew what I had to do. Chris fenced her semifinal bout before I fenced mine. She finished third and didn't make the gold-medal final. I knew I had to win my semifinal bout. If I did, I would finish the season number one and make the world championship team. My whole year was on the line.

I was fencing Nicole Mustilli and she was killing me. We fence a 15-touch bout; the first one to 15 wins. She had

14 and I had 7. Everybody thought I was history, and I felt like I was standing on the edge of a cliff and if I took one step backward everything would be gone. I had a coach at one end of the strip and a coach at the other end of the strip. The one behind me is yelling at me not to look at the scoreboard. He said, "Fence this touch. Don't look at the scoreboard," and the other one's yelling, "Look at the scoreboard!" So naturally I looked at the scoreboard.

I knew where I was, but I knew the battle wasn't over because I felt I could step back, reach down inside, and fight. At 14–7, I stepped back from the line and tried to find one touch, one action. I stepped up to the line and began to fight. I scored one touch. I stepped back and didn't look at the scoreboard again. I was fighting for one touch. I was fighting for everything right there, each touch.

The dynamics of the battle immediately changed when I took it to 14–8. In that touch I knew I could do it, I knew I could win. Also, I felt my opponent change at that point. I felt she was no longer fighting to win. She was fighting not to lose.

She changed how she approached me on the strip, which worked to my advantage. When I'm in a bout and I stop fighting to win and start fighting not to lose, I'm almost guaranteed to lose because I quit taking chances. I quit risking. I get conservative. You plan on your opponent not making a mistake instead of forcing her to make a mistake. So touch by touch I fought my way back and ended up winning 15–14.

Sports are very emotional. The emotion is there because you're putting every ounce of energy you have on the line. So when I was on the strip in that championship bout there was a lot of emotion. I'd worked for ten years to get to that point, and with one touch I could watch it shift to someone else.

It would have been so easy to allow the expectations to interfere with what I had to do. That's when you look at what you have to lose and what you have to prove. If I feel like I have to prove myself to you on the strip, then I have something to lose and it makes it difficult for me to perform.

The scariest opponent for me in the tournament was Nicole, because she had absolutely nothing to lose, nothing to prove. Going in, nobody expected her to beat me. If she did, she would be a hero; if she didn't, that would be okay because nobody expected it. That's what made her scary. That's what makes any opponent scary.

When the score was 14–7 she changed. Up to that point she had dominated everything, but then she realized she could win. She just needed one more point. When she suddenly realized she could win, she began trying not to lose.

My toughest defeat was a 15–14 loss in Switzerland in 1998 in the finals of the first ever World Championship event in women's saber. Saber is a cutting-edge weapon. You hit with the edge of the blade and not with the point. It's like you're slapped with the blade, so there is a fair amount of surface pain. That's probably why they didn't allow women to fence saber internationally for so long. It's always been considered a man's weapon, too brutal for women. The dynamics of the bout are very different. It's much faster because of the way the touches are earned.

In the final, I was fencing Donna Saworski from Canada. There really wasn't a favorite because it was such a

new event and we were untested at that level. I was very
nervous going in. I believed that technically and tactically I
was a better, stronger fencer. My coach was not with me,
but I did have the support of the rest of the team.

Because I was nervous I was moving too fast and I
was too tense. My actions were too big and she jumped
out to a lead. Then I matched her lead. She'd take the lead
again and I would match it again. It got to a point where
she was ahead 14–10, one point away from becoming
world champion.

I stepped back and told myself, "You've been here
before; you can do this; it's not impossible." A lot of people
think it's too big a gap to bridge, but I knew it was possible because of what I had done in the National
Championship. I knew I had it within me to find a way to
win. So that's where I began. Touch by touch, I came back
to close the gap and reached 14–14.

It was down to one touch, and the final action was
what we call a simultaneous action, where both fencers
attack at the same time. When this happens, as long as both
fencers land, no one scores a touch. You basically ignore
each other's touch. But the position of her blade closed out
my blade and only one light registered on the machine. She
hit me and I didn't hit her. It was over. It was a touch that
could have gone either way, and it went in her favor; she
closed me out on the attack. I don't think she even meant
to; it was just where her blade was in her attack. To see only
one light on the machine deflated me, because I really felt
I could have won. It was my toughest loss.

I don't know if I'll ever really get over it, but I've
learned to look at it a little differently, in the light of what

I was *able to do* as opposed to what I *didn't* do. What I did do was bring home a silver medal from the World Championship, which no American had ever done. But for the longest time all I could see was, I didn't bring home the gold. ■

"One bout doesn't make a champion. One win or one loss isn't reflective of an entire career. I've had a lot of challenges, and champions aren't made or lost with one battle."

KELLY WILLIAMS

"I actually enjoy failing because I learn more about myself as a person and as a competitor when I fail than when I win."

AMY VAN DYKEN,
Olympic gold-medalist swimmer

"You've always got to be aware of why you don't win, otherwise you'll keep losing. Every mistake is a learning experience, and hopefully you won't make the same mistake again."

LAYNE BEACHLEY,
world surfing champion

"It's easy to say success is having a gold medal or winning a championship, but I think it is much more than that. It's being able to know I did absolutely everything I could possibly do to win. The results are less significant than the effort."

KELLY WILLIAMS,
U.S. national saber champion

Bonnie BLAIR

My 1993 season was really a difficult one. The clock wasn't reading what I wanted it to. Things just weren't clicking, and I started wondering, Am I over the hill? Has time run out on me? A part of me didn't think so, yet I knew something wasn't right. It was a constant struggle all season long.

What got me through 1993 was the love I have for speed skating. Had I not had that love I would have been so frustrated, I would have just said, "Forget it. This isn't worth it. Maybe I am over the hill. I'll just leave."

But my love for the sport

Speed skater Bonnie Blair is the winningest U.S. athlete in Olympic Winter Games history, with six medals, five of them gold. She has been honored with the Sullivan Award and the Flo Hyman Award and was named Sports Illustrated's Sportsman of the Year in 1994. Bonnie says the Calgary Olympics in 1988 were special. Not only did she win her first Olympic gold medal in the 500-meter, she won it by breaking a world record that had been set just minutes before by one of her competitors. Bonnie said, "It was a compelling, moving moment that's hard to capture again. There's definitely a lot to be said for the first time." In addition to her successes, Bonnie, like all great athletes, had down times when she was tested but never gave up.

would keep pushing me out there every single day to try to figure out what was wrong, fix it, and then get back to being the athlete I knew I could be. It was a season with a lot of frustration, but the next year I came back and had one of the best years I've ever had. I like to think sticking to it paid off, but I also know a great part was really based on the love I have for the sport. ∎

"I'm not glad I fell, but I'm glad I fought for it, that I didn't stomp off like a baby. I hope at these Olympics people will remember me for how hard I tried, not how great I did."

NICOLE BOBEK,

U.S. figure skater who finished seventeenth at Nagano, landing only two of nine jumps and falling twice in her long program

Claire CARVER-DIAS

The leading member of Canada's national synchronized swimming team, Claire says, "My top priority is the duet and the team because they are Olympic events." But she still plans to swim solo at major competitions. Canada won first place in duet and team at the 1999 Pan Am Games—a gold medal sweep.

I was a skinny, gangly, awkward kid, but I had a coach who kept telling me I had talent. He said there was something special about what I did, and I believe it was because I liked what I was doing. That's what made it special for me.

Liking what you do is hugely important. It gives you an extra drive that keeps you from being just mediocre and makes you excel. Because I like synchronized swimming, it gives me that extra little edge, so when people watch me they enjoy it because it looks like I like performing. It looks like I'm having fun. I am. ∎

"Identify your personal limits and then push past them. Then set new barriers, and repeat the process, again and again and again."

NICOLE HAISLETT,
winner of three gold medals in swimming in the 1992 Olympic Games

Lori
BELANGER

Lori grew up in Wingham, Ontario, population 2,952. Wingham was the first town in Canada to have both a radio station and a television station. Lori's father worked at the television station so she always followed him there, saw all the things he did, and decided at an early age that she loved the business.

After graduating from college with a broadcasting degree, she followed her passion of basketball and joined the broadcast production team of the NBA Toronto Raptors. Her next stop was Global Television, where she became their first full-fledged female sports reporter and anchor.

My biggest dose of reality since I've been in this particular position is having people I want to hire me say right to my face, "I don't think you're good. I don't like you." I overcame that the first time because I had already figured this out from the person's tone and body language, so I didn't really get upset. But it's hard to just sit there and listen. I would retreat a little bit into my shell. But I decided I just needed to get better at what I was doing and then wait for the next opportunity because I'm not going to change this person's mind. If he doesn't like me, that's a bit of a road block, so I'll have to approach him later when one of us has changed.

Right now I'm in the process of trying to improve areas of my on-air presence that I don't think I'm great at, in order to satisfy my own assessment of myself. I've always set my goals really high, and the essential tool in being able to reach those goals is being competitive enough to want them. I try to realize that everything is subjective anyway. If one news director doesn't like me, another news director will. ∎

"I honestly think that everyone has weaknesses. The strongest person you see in a day may be the one going home and crying himself to sleep at night."

LORI BELANGER

Joan
BENOIT
SAMUELSON

The gold medalist in the first women's Olympic Marathon in 1984, Joan recalls that when she came into the Los Angeles Coliseum and saw all the colors, flags, and fans, she told herself, "Listen, just look straight ahead, because if you don't, you're probably going to faint." The next year Joan set another American record, running the Chicago Marathon in 2:21:21.

My first masters competition was in the Chicago Marathon. I ran with the lead pack for the first few miles, and they were running very fast. So I dropped back and figured to pick people off as best I could. I thought the lead pack was really strong and tight, and that speaks well for the sport.

At about 8 or 9 miles, I felt a twinge in my left calf but thought I might be able to work it out. At 11 miles it seized and it was like I was shot out of the water. I felt like a bullet went through me.

I stopped and looked for a therapist or a medic, but I couldn't find anyone so I made it to the halfway point. When I got there I had the calf massaged. The medic asked if I'd ever run a marathon before, and I said, "Yeah, a few times."

I probably should have dropped out at 13 miles, but I

have two kids at home whom I tell to finish whatever they start. This was my first marathon as a master, and I did finish. Chicago has a special place in my heart. I'll be back. ■

"The harder you work, the harder it is to surrender."

PAT SUMMITT,
women's basketball coach at Tennessee—six-time national champions

"You can't measure success if you have never failed."

STEFFI GRAF,
winner of twenty-two Grand Slam tennis titles

Charmaine
HOOPER

Charmaine was born in Guyana and lived in Lusaka, Zambia, for almost three years, where her father was a Canadian diplomat. At the International School in Zambia, she started playing soccer. Moving to Canada in 1978, Charmaine played tennis, hockey, and most other sports, but she always returned to soccer. She played collegiate soccer at North Carolina State, where she was an All-American and won the H.C. Kennett Award as outstanding female athlete. Charmaine also lived and played soccer in Japan for four years, where she was named league MVP. She is a member of the Canadian women's national soccer team and toured with the World All-Star team.

I'm definitely not afraid of winning. I think that comes from the fact that playing for Canada—I'm not putting Canada down, but playing for Canada I've lost a lot of games in my career. This is really bad to admit but maybe I've come to accept losing a little bit more than I have in the past. It's not because I want to lose—no way, I want to win. Every time I go out there I'm very competitive. But after you've lost so many games you may come to accept losing, and that's a bad thing.

Every time I've played the United States, we've lost. Every

time we come up against the Americans I'm competitive, because I'm sick of losing to them. The Americans have money to do what they're doing, they have money to give them the opportunity to be better players. I'm a little envious. These players have a lot of endorsements and sponsorships. Whereas, if you look at Canada, we have almost nothing. Whenever I go out to play against the United States, I want to show that I am just as good or better than these U.S. players, and that alone makes me more competitive playing against them.

I want to do well for myself. I mean that even though my team isn't doing well, I want to make sure I'm doing well. Maybe that's what drives me. For the last eight years I've been in Chicago training with men's teams every year. I think that keeps me going. I'm always striving to be better than the men I'm playing against; I'm always striving not to be the worst player out there. Whenever I get out and play with the national team I remind myself that I've been training with men who are better than the women I'm going to be playing against. So I should be able to come out and do well. That's one way I try to look at it. ∎

"You should enjoy what you are doing, and if you enjoy what you are doing you are going to do well, and then you'll get better at it."

CHARMAINE HOOPER

JJ ISLER

JJ is among the top women sailors in the world. She is a three-time world champion, won a 1992 Olympic bronze medal in the 470 class, and was named Rolex Yachtswoman of the Year. She was on the **Mighty Mary** *all-women's team in the 1995 America's Cup. As proficient a sailor as she is, JJ actually fell out of a boat while racing in Baltimore Harbor. There was a big wind shift and she was leaning too far out of the boat. Because of the pollution in the harbor, racing was suspended until JJ was taken ashore and made to shower and clean off. Competition then resumed, and she won. Like all outstanding athletes, JJ has had her share of triumphs and disappointments, but she has never given up.*

My biggest disappointment was being taken off the America's Cup race boat in 1995. I was benched in the last round of racing on the *Mighty Mary.* It had been an all-women's team, but Bill Koch replaced me with Dave Dellenbaugh, one of the male coaches.

I had been the starting helmsman and tactician. I would steer at the start, when the boats circle and do that dogfight. Once we crossed the starting line, I would hand off the helm to Leslie Egnot, and then as tactician I would make the decisions as to where we would go on the racecourse. I would be the one calling every tack and jibe.

We started the competition by sailing the boat that won in 1992. The America's Cup is a complete design game, and we brought the oldest car to the racetrack. I felt we had been performing respectfully. We were out there against teams who had a lot more experience than we did, and they all had new boats. We got ours, the *Mighty Mary*, very late in the program. We really needed for this boat to be significantly faster than our old boat in order for us to win, but it wasn't. It showed potential. There were times it was quite fast, but it was a very tricky boat to sail.

As tactician you're in the hot seat, and when your team's not winning, it's one of two things: either the boat is slow and you're stuck with it, or you're sending the boat the wrong way. Tacticians are always replaceable. Nonetheless, it was pretty tough to be told to sit on the bench, and it was especially difficult being replaced by a male coach, because this meant our all-women's team concept fell apart. We had wonderful camaraderie, and we were showing the world we could compete equally.

The team always met at 5:45 A.M. to go for our morning run. As we headed out the door, Bill Koch tapped me on the shoulder and told me he'd decided to put me on the bench and replace me with Dave Dellenbaugh, that day and for the rest of the series. I don't think you know how you're going to react to something so completely unexpected, but for whatever reason, I thought this was that huge wind shift I had been waiting for. So I was able to stay pretty calm at first. Then when the team came back from the run he told everyone, and at that point it got pretty difficult. A lot of people started crying. One team member said she felt like she'd just been kicked in the gut.

Stu Argo, one of the male coaches, gave me the best piece of advice. He said, "You've got to find a niche for yourself, and you've got to be productive. That's what's going to make it or break it for you. If you stay with the team, you're going to have to feel that you're contributing." The tough thing is, we were in the semifinals and all the focus was on the A team, so he was really right. I had to create my own niche. I had to make myself useful. No one was going to do it for me.

Initially, I just switched jobs with Dave and became one of the coaches. I would go out on the big tender and listen on the radio. We had four or five boats up the course giving weather data and a helicopter giving additional weather reports. I would sit next to the team meteorologist, and we'd crunch through all the different weather readings and his forecast and turn that into a game plan Dave could use for deciding, basically, whether to go left or to go right. So I was still looking at all those variables and I remained an integral part of the decision making for the team.

One thing I learned was that if I was ever on another A team I would really have a much better feel for how to treat the back-up team. It's a tough job to be back-up. You truly need to have a B team, and you need to make those team members feel they have a constructive role. You also have to give them an honest assessment of what their chances are to make the A team. And at the same time you've got to give them their dream, their reason for doing it.

The important thing to remember is, when you're told to sit on the bench, that's what you need to do—go sit on the bench. I'm proud of myself that I didn't quit. It would have been so easy, especially with an eighteen-month-old daughter at home, to say, "I really owe it to my family to leave," and take off. I'm really glad I stuck it out, even when it was obvious I wasn't going to get back on the A team.

After you're told by your coach to sit on the bench, you need to make yourself useful. Maybe you can fill some role and help the coach with some duty, such as mapping out the game plan or keeping track of stats of what the other team is doing. There were times the coaches would want to relay something to the A team and I would hop on the race boat and explain it because we figured it would work better coming from a member of the team. I tried to make myself useful as kind of a junior coach, which was a great learning experience.

Another thing I learned was the importance of keeping my opinion of the decision to myself. I didn't give any interviews for a long time. It was important to calm the whole team and continue to be a team player. ■

"We have the misconception that competitiveness means winning at all costs, but that's not what competition is. Competition is just doing your best and not giving up. We all face a moment in a race or in a competition in which we want to give up. We can either give in and not keep pushing, or we can charge forward and work through it. Teaching a child how to work through discomfort is great. It's very fulfilling. I get tired of so many parents saying competition is bad. It's not. You can make competition fun for kids as long as they have their priorities straight."

LISA RAINSBERGER,
winning marathoner

Michelle
AKERS

Michelle is the starting central midfielder of the U.S. women's national soccer team, the 1999 Women's World Cup champions. Michele is the first and only woman to receive FIFA's highest honor, the Order of Merit, for her positive contributions to the game. In late 1991, just a few weeks after leading the U.S. national team to its first World Cup soccer title, she was stricken with an extremely debilitating case of CFIDS (chronic fatigue immune dysfunction syndrome). Her battle against this devastating disease has been long and arduous.

I felt like I was in hell. At my worst I was barely able to complete day-to-day activities. Little chores knocked me out for days or weeks. I was a total mess. But my illness challenged me enormously to be vulnerable and share my heart. Before I had to be Superwoman and be guarded, never to cry in front of people, never to show my hurts. Well, I learned you can't be like that all the time.

It was exhausting to fight my body to appear normal and then try to play soccer at the highest level. After years of battling the illness and trying to maintain my status on the national team, I finally gave up. I fell to my knees and cried to God, "I can't do this anymore. I have no more strength."

And God turned my suffering into a blessing and a miracle. CFIDS has been a blessing; it enabled me to find out who I am. I thought I had all the answers. I thought I had the strength and the means to know joy, happiness, and success in life. Boy, was I wrong! When all my efforts failed and I stood alone looking for something to bail me out, I was forced to acknowledge the fact that there is something more to life than me and my now inadequate resources.

I thought, I can't just be here to win soccer trophies and championships. When it's all said and done, who really cares if you're the best in the world? Through struggles and defeat, not triumph, we create an intimate bond between people. It's amazing to me that a situation that brings you to your knees, and causes you to feel immense pain, whether emotional, physical, or spiritual, can be the overriding link between each of us. Defining moments in my life have come in the struggle to overcome. It's the struggle that makes you triumphant. It's not necessarily the medal around your neck that makes you a champion. I'm eternally grateful for the illness. If it weren't for the darkness, I would never have been able to see the stars. ■

SIX

FACE YOUR FEARS

"When I'm up on the hill I have moments of fear. I'm human, and when I look at a course there are times when I say, 'Wow, that's hairy,' and I'm afraid of that part of the course. But what you do is face that fear with the task at hand and then you don't have the fear, because fear is nonproductive. Just wheels spinning."

PICABO STREET,
Olympic gold medal skier

Aimee MULLINS

Aimee was born without fibula bones, and because of this, her legs were amputated below the knee when she was a year old. As a teen Aimee swam, played soccer, skied, and biked. She ran track for Georgetown University and has held three world track and field records for below-the-knee double amputees. She started a promising career as a fashion model, opening Alexander McQueen's London Fashion Week show for Givenchy, and was named one of **People** *magazine's "50 Most Beautiful People." Aimee says, "The truth is, I'm sort of lucky to have this body, because it forced me to find my strength and beauty within."*

I'm proud that I somehow found the where-with-all to go out for track at Georgetown University, that I made the leap and didn't look back. I went for the gusto and swallowed my pride, pride in the sense that you're afraid of failing. What singles out the successful athlete from the ones who never make it past a plateau is that successful athletes do it anyway, even though they are terrified. That's why I'm so proud. I just did it.

I called up Coach Frank Gagliano, and my career went from there. I had no background whatsoever in track. I knew nothing. It wasn't until my first race that I knew how far 200 meters was. I had been on my new sprinting legs (prostheses), which were prototypes, for about a month. However, we hadn't seen how they performed in different weather.

We were at Villanova, and it was the first really hot muggy day of the season. I was to run both the 100 and the 200. I had silicone sleeves over my knees that had a latex feel to them. When you sweat in something like that, the sweat acts like a lubricant between your skin and the latex, so about 85 meters into the 100-meter race I almost came out of my right leg. I just totally flipped out. I finished with the leg intact, but barely. I'm sure it would have come off if I had kept going at top speed.

When you're sprinting, the last thing you want to be thinking about is your leg coming off. If it almost came off at 85 meters, I knew it was not going to stay on for 200. This was a big championship, with loads of people in the stands. Having my legs fall off seemed to be the most humiliating thing I would ever face. There was no way I was going to run the 200. I had run only a couple of meets on those funky-looking legs. I was terrified. People from the other schools, the other competitors, were just getting used to me. Word had spread that I was going to run for Georgetown, and now I had to deal with this whole other factor. It was one thing to get on the track in those legs, but it was another if I came out of them during the race, because a couple of hundred spectators were likely to faint.

I begged Coach Gagliano to scratch me from the 200. I told him, "I can't go through with this; I know my leg's going to come off." He refused to hear my plea. I literally got down on my knees and begged, "Don't you understand?" I couldn't fathom why he didn't see this was going to be the most embarrassing moment in my life. He just stared at me and barked out the kind of pep talk only coaches know how to make at these crucial moments: "So what if your leg falls off? If it falls off, you fall down, you pick it up, you put it back on, you get up, and you finish the goddamn race."

I was like, Oh, my God, I can't believe this!

It was truly that simple. What is the worst thing that can happen? Your leg comes off, you fall down, you put your leg back on, get up, and keep running. It's a great metaphor for life. But at the time it was very unnerving. My race definitely wasn't glamorous. I didn't go full speed because I wanted to keep my legs on at all costs. I barely made it around the track. My time was pathetic, but at least Gag smiled at me because I ran the damn thing. He's one of the best people I have ever met. Everyone should have a Frank Gagliano in her life.

I cringe when I'm told, "Oh, Aimee, you're such a motivational, inspirational person!" So many speakers get up and say things like, "I was never afraid to fail . . . I was never afraid to try . . . I never thought of not making it . . . I never cared what people thought of me." That's all a bunch of crap, because everyone is afraid.

Everyone wants to be awesome and look awesome; everyone is really afraid of getting out there and not being good. That's the challenge. To be afraid and know people are staring at you and know you might not do all that well—but you do it anyway. I think that's a really powerful thing, especially for kids.

People don't explore anymore, because no one's forcing them to do it. So when you finally do find something you want to try, it's terrifying. It is so easy to quit. I am such a competitive, proud person. To get on that track at Georgetown every time knowing I was going to lose was tough. Those were the hardest times of my life.

I think I did it because it was so hard I couldn't walk away. I couldn't sleep at night, knowing there was something out there that scared the hell out of me and I had backed down. ∎

"Winners keep going even when they are afraid. They test what they are made of. They trust themselves, and they believe in themselves."

AIMEE MULLINS

"Every single meet when they say 'on your mark'—that feeling in my stomach and my throat: it's like the first time I ever ran. I always think, Why am I doing this? It's so nerve-racking. I can't sleep the night before. But as soon as the race is over I can't wait to do it again. Running is like a test of will."

AIMEE MULLINS

Michele MITCHELL-ROCHA

Michele is the diving coach at the University of Arizona. She says, "I got my coaching philosophy from my parents because they always reminded me I was diving because I enjoyed it. Whatever happened, they supported me. My dad would hug me when I had tears because I hadn't lived up to my own goals. He and my mom would emphasize that I was doing the sport for me, not them. This really comes out of me as a coach."

Fear is a part of the sport of platform diving. It's part of mastering the sport, and it's part of the thrill of the sport. You're 33 feet up, and not only do you have to perform the skill but you have to do it so high off the water. Yes, there's a huge fear factor; there were times in my career when I was almost paralyzed by it.

What you're afraid of is getting lost in your dive and landing on your back instead of going in the water vertically. Any diver who's ever gotten lost and landed flat on the water knows why that fear is so great. It's like someone took a two-by-four and slammed you in the middle of your back. It creates very painful bruises. I landed so flat a couple of times I was coughing up blood. The impact force is pretty significant if you don't do it right. ∎

"There's always a point in our sport when you just have to jump off the cliff and see what's going to happen."

MICHELE MITCHELL-ROCHA

"The first time I got in a race car as a driver, I was scared to death. But eventually fear is not a factor. You file it away. There is a line you step over where you have, totally in your mind, dealt with every possible safety issue. Once you cross over that line you don't think about those things. They are just not an issue."

LYN ST. JAMES, *Indy car driver*

Sylvie BERNIER

Sylvie is a Canadian diver who took up the sport as a youngster because of severe asthma. She grew up loving the circus, especially all of the somersaults. Sylvie spent a lot of time on her parents' mattress, playing circus, practicing flips, and breaking the legs of the bed. She even did somersaults from the roof of the house into snowdrifts. Sylvie just liked being in the air, and her parents said, "Why not try diving?" That's how it started, and it has never stopped.

I think the fear is always there. At the beginning it's the fear when you try new dives: the fear of the board, the fear of hurting yourself, the fear of landing flat in the water, the fear of getting lost during the dive. It's a sport where you have to orient yourself in the air. You always have a fear that if you're tired one day, you wonder, Am I going to get lost? When the years go by the fear changes. It's just the fear of missing your dive, the fear of not competing at the level you want to. Diving is a sport that keeps you on the edge all the time. That's why I was always in tune to my feelings. For instance, if I was tired or if I didn't feel well, I was always trying not to push myself so I wouldn't get hurt.

When you spin in the air and you do somersaults, you always have to know where you are. We call it spotting. You spot the water, you spot the roof—or the sky, if you're outdoors. If you get lost it's very scary. For a fraction of a second, you have no idea where you are. That means you're in trouble. That's why early on, when I moved to Montreal, I really learned how to spot and to never lose a second of concentration. I always knew exactly where I was. But that takes a lot of time and lots of work on the trampoline with the belt. You do your dives, your somersaults, and then you spot. You must learn how to spot. That's exactly what I did the last two years of competition. It was very important for me to work on consistency, and to work on consistency means you always have to do a good dive. The minimum score had to be 7. For that you have to know exactly where you are in the air. ■

"If you're on the pool deck, be on the pool deck mentally and physically."

SYLVIE BERNIER

Chris
WITTY

Chris was America's only double medalist in the 1998 Nagano Winter Olympics, capturing a silver and a bronze in speed skating. Three Olympic goals remain: first, to win a gold medal in speed skating; second, to medal in cycling; and third, to win a gold medal in both speed skating and cycling. Chris says, "It's easier to limit yourself, but if you do, you will never reach your full potential."

I am afraid of failure, but I think that's a good thing. If you're afraid, you'll do what you can *not* to fail. You learn from your failures, because they're going to happen. Everybody who is successful has failed sometime.

One of the hardest things for me was growing up in a family that wasn't financially stable. My dad ended up losing his job when I was younger, and I almost quit the sport because of it. I had to miss out on skating meets and skate on used skates that didn't fit. It was hard to handle.

I went to training camp, and everybody else would be going to a movie but I couldn't because the five dollars in my pocket had to last the rest of the week. There was peer pressure about not being able to do what other kids got to do. But physically I've been blessed, and I'm fortunate to be a natural athlete, so I tried to use that the best I could.

Speed skating isn't a sport with a lot of money, and we don't have any opportunity to move to a professional level. We don't do it for the money. We don't do it for fame and fortune. We do it because we love to do it. ∎

"A competitor is a person who hates
to lose and who will do anything
she can to win, not just to beat
other people, but to improve herself.
A winner is somebody who's
accomplished all her goals and done
everything she set out to do."

CHRIS WITTY

Joy FAWCETT

One of the best soccer defenders in the world, Joy is a twelve-year veteran of the U.S. national team that won both the 1991 and 1999 World Cup. In the 1996 Atlanta Olympics, she played every minute in all five games during the team's gold medal performance. Her energy is just as prevalent off the field—"Mama Joy," as her teammates call her, is the mother of two daughters, Katey, six, and Carli, three. The girls lived with their mom near the team's training site before the 1999 World Cup, and their presence constantly reminded players of the importance of keeping everything in its proper perspective.

I have some fear of failing, but if you let it overtake you, you're not going to get anywhere. You're not going to challenge yourself. You don't want to fail, but you're not going to accomplish anything if you don't take that chance. It's hard to push this fear out of your mind, but when you achieve your small goals, these keep you going. You gain confidence and you feel good about yourself, and that will help you overcome the fear of failure.

My biggest obstacle was self-confidence. I didn't always have a lot of faith in myself. It's a big problem for me. I wouldn't say I have as many doubts as I used to, but

I still have them. My doubts are caused by a lot of things, but dealing with them has resulted in where I am today. I'm always striving to get better.

When self-doubt enters my mind I try to tell myself, All you can do is your best. Give it everything you can and, whether you make it or not, you've tried your best. If you've done that, there's nothing else you can give, and you should be proud of yourself. ■

"People get paralyzed when they become really successful because they start thinking, 'I don't want to fail.' You have to keep attacking, putting yourself in situations where you could possibly fail. You have to stick your neck out where you could take a fall."

GABRIELLE REECE,
pro beach volleyball star

"When you're motivated by fear, your perspective is really limited because all you're doing is trying to survive."

VIRGINIA SAVAGE,
sports psychologist

"I always ran chased by the fear of being beaten. It brought out the best in me."

SHIRLEY STRICKLAND,
winner of seven Olympic medals,
including three golds, in track for Australia

"What is fear? Everyone is frightened the first time. But if the coach knows how to prepare, you won't be afraid."

OLGA KORBUT,
gymnastics star of the 1972
Munich Olympics with one gold
and two silver medals

Debi THOMAS

Debi was the 1986 world figure skating champion, but "Debi" is not the original spelling of her name. As a youngster she dreamed of stardom, so she shortened her name for autographs. But that was only part of it. Debi says, "I mainly changed it because I didn't like writing two bs next to each other because they never matched. That's how compulsive I am about some things. I thought the b's just didn't look right; they weren't the same. So I got rid of one b and thought I might as well get rid of the e too."

I've never been afraid of failure, so I don't know how to tell somebody who is afraid of failure how not to be afraid. I usually think of the worst thing that can happen. Am I going to die from this? No. The worst that can happen is I can be really embarrassed but I'm not going to die from it. To me, never trying feels a lot worse than failing. But I'll tell you, failing does not feel too good either.

I've been through some periods of time when I felt I was a big loser, but I know darn well I'm not. You don't achieve what I have by being a big loser. But even someone who has accomplished great things sometimes feels like a big loser because of failure. The difference is, you can overcome failure.

If I fail at something, I try everything in my power to figure out why it happened and what I'm going to do to keep it from ever happening again. Sometimes it takes a long time. It's very difficult. ■

"I tell people the reason I've accomplished so much is, 'I'm too stupid to know what's impossible.' That's an original Debi Thomas quote."

DEBI THOMAS

"I don't fear failure. I don't accept it. I don't even think about failure. It's not in my dictionary."

TERA CRISMAN,
world champion jet skier

Nancy
LOPEZ

"Golf is a sport you can't control and can't conquer," Nancy says. "Golf is frustrating, just like life." She once asked her dad about her follow-through. She was upset because it didn't feel right. "Nancy," her dad replied, "It doesn't make any difference to a golf ball what you do after you hit it."

Fear of failure drives me competitively, probably more so in the last few years. I want to play well, because I don't know how many good rounds I have left in me.

When I was younger I wasn't afraid to fail, because I hadn't failed very much. I didn't really know what failure was. I just kept playing aggressively, the best I could. If I didn't make a putt or win the tournament, I was almost surprised at myself. I wasn't afraid to fail at all. ■

"A champion is afraid of losing.
Everyone else is afraid of winning."

BILLIE JEAN KING,
*holder of a record twenty
Wimbledon tennis titles*

"Fear isn't some dramatic horror
that comes along in one shot. It's the
constant fear of not meeting the
challenge of giving your best every
moment. The only way to stand
against it is to concentrate all your
energy on every run, top to bottom."

KATE MCBRIDE,
*world champion downhill
ski endurance racer*

"It's okay to be scared, but don't let
it dictate your actions."

MICHELLE AKERS,
*member of the U.S. national soccer team,
1999 Women's World Cup champions*

Suzie
MCCONNELL
SERIO

Suzie, a mother of four, is currently an outstanding guard in the WNBA. At Penn State, she was an All-American and holds the NCAA all-time assist record with 1,307. Suzie played on two U.S. Olympic basketball teams. In the Serio household "she got next" refers to bath time. Suzie is a coach in the off season. In 1993 she took the girls of Pittsburgh's Oakland Catholic High to the Pennsylvania state championship. Suzie is certainly a testament to "You can do anything you want to do."

Anytime we do something that's important, we have a fear of failing. When you have that fear you have a choice. You either give up and don't pursue it because you're afraid to fail or you work harder and continue to believe in yourself and in your abilities. That's the choice I chose to make because I don't like to give in to anything. When my back's against the wall or when I'm an underdog, I love a challenge. That's when I rise to the occasion. ■

"I think most people who are successful do fear failure, but it's a matter of, What is failure? Is it because you lost a game, or is it because you missed a shot, or is it because you never got off the bench? Is it failure not to be a starter? What is failure? It's all in other people's eyes. That's where we get caught up in what other people think."

ANNIE MEYERS
DRYSDALE,
member, Basketball Hall of Fame

Adriana DUFFY

Adriana is the Puerto Rican gymnast who, while competing at the 1989 World Gymnastics Championships, slipped on a vault and dislocated her neck, paralyzing her from mid-chest down. Since then, Adriana has earned degrees from Stanford University and Yale Law School, and she is an attorney with a prominent San Francisco law firm. Adriana has never been tempted to ask, "Why me?" As she says, "That's a question that has never made sense to me, like the question, 'Why not?'"

She adds, "That's just not the way the world works."

Would I vault again? That's a good question. There are times when I think no and there are times when I think yes. I go back and forth. Clearly, gymnastics is a sport that has risks. But lots of things have risks; one is driving a car.

My accident has made me think more about the safety of gymnastics and whether some things are too dangerous. I think it's probably a good thing to examine, not that one shouldn't do gymnastics or any other sport that carries a certain amount of risk, but to know what the risks are. On the other hand, if you're performing with fear, you're more likely to get hurt. So, it's a double-edged sword. ■

"If people are impressed because they think I should be moping around the house being depressed about my life, they just don't get it. My life is full. I've done a lot of things. I don't feel any desire to have anybody else's life."

ADRIANA DUFFY

SEVEN

BELIEVE IN YOURSELF

"You have to believe in yourself. The ones who believe in themselves the most are the ones who win."

FLORENCE GRIFFITH-JOYNER,

winner of three gold medals in track and field in the 1988 Seoul Olympics

Julie FOUDY

Julie grew up in Mission Viejo, California, where everyone—girls and boys—played soccer. There were many organized leagues and lots of good coaching. Her parents were her role models because they were very supportive, despite knowing nothing about soccer. Her mom still doesn't know what position she plays. However, they let her make her own decisions about where she wanted to go with it, and Julie thinks that's critical for kids.

Winners have confidence. When I go into a game I know there's no way we'll lose because there's this feeling inside that I've done everything I can do. I've totally prepared. I'm ready. It's a wonderful feeling, especially when you put in so many hours and so much sweat and tears, to say, "I walk the walk, now it's time to show everyone. It's show time." That's how the Olympics were. People asked if we were surprised that we won the gold. It was like, Hell, no. We knew we were going to win the gold. That's what we were there for.

A winner expects to win. If you look at the top teams in soccer, physically we all match up. It's the little things that make such a difference, and the mind-set of a team is foremost. It's everything. It's a feeling of invincibility for me. I'm on the field, and I get an adrenaline rush that makes me think

I cannot lose. I have so much energy and so much adrenaline running through me, I feel almost superhuman. ■

"We feel we are on the brink of something great. It transcends soccer. There's a bigger message out there: When people tell you, 'No,' just smile and tell them, 'Yes, I can.'"

JULIE FOUDY

"Winners rise to the challenge of the competition, and mentally they don't let things get them down. They think positively and go in with that mind-set."

JOY FAWCETT,
member of U.S. national soccer team,
considered to be the world's best
woman defender

Silken
LAUMANN

Silken is a four-time Olympic rower. But her story is far more than a sports story. Silken survived broken bones and shredded muscles to achieve Olympic glory. She epitomizes courage, perseverance, and triumph of the human spirit. Silken has developed powerful tools for realizing excellence— vision, focus, and commitment. When applied consistently, these tools empower individuals to reach their own potential.

In order to be good at something, so much effort is required that you must find joy in what you do. You truly have to love what you're doing. I really believe this applies in any area of life. If you are finding joy in it, it still takes work, but it doesn't feel as much like work.

For some reason, we are rarely told that people fail and that those who eventually succeed have failed many times before. So when a young person meets with her first failure, she often gets very discouraged. I say to young women that failure and missed attempts are just the process of success. Don't waste time second-guessing yourself, or not having confidence. Just try as hard as you can to see your failures as learning experiences and as natural parts of your eventual success. It took me a long time to learn that one.

Ultimately, you have to do it for yourself. You've got to race for yourself; you've got to find something in your efforts that has meaning to you. Only you can define that. And once you have a really clear idea of why you are doing something, you are going to be much more at peace with yourself. ∎

"As long as I can focus on enjoying what I'm doing, having fun, I know I'll play well."

STEFFI GRAF,
twenty-two time Grand Slam
tennis champion

Charmaine
HOOPER

Charmaine is the all-time leading goal scorer for the Canadian women's national soccer team. She is a fierce competitor and is regarded as one of the best players in the world. Charmaine feels that physical fitness is part of her success and says, "I will challenge any guy to do dips, pull-ups, and push-ups any day."

One thing I try to tell the girls I work with is believe in yourself. Even if they don't feel confident, I think they can always find something good within themselves. Maybe they're a fast runner, or they're very fit, or they have a certain move that works for them. There's something good they can find within themselves to give them a little bit of confidence and help them believe in themselves a little bit more. Even if they're down on their whole game, there is something they have, some quality about themselves that would help them be more confident. ■

"At eighteen years old, I thought I had peaked and I didn't see myself getting any better. But now, at thirty-one, I'm still becoming better each time I go out there. That's what keeps me going, knowing I can still play and I can still play well."

CHARMAINE HOOPER

Carol
HEISS
JENKINS

Carol remembers when she heard her name announced as the 1960 Winter Olympic Games ladies figure skating champion. It was the first time she had heard it said aloud, and to climb up on the top step of the podium, she recalls, was a feeling that's very difficult to describe. When the anthem was played and the American flag was raised in her honor, she had tears in her eyes and a big smile on her face.

I never thought about not winning. I don't think that's conceit because there's a fine line between being conceited and having confidence in yourself. Conceit is thinking you can do it without hard work and perseverance. However, you need a certain amount of self-confidence, because if you don't have that self-confidence you're not going to win.

I think the highly competitive are born that way. I don't think it's something you can learn. I can see it in the little kids. The ones who are highly competitive say, "I'm not getting off this ice until I do that jump at least one time." They're the ones who can really combat the nerves. ∎

BELIEVE IN YOURSELF 171

Debi THOMAS

Debi tells about the time she was working with her new choreographer, George De La Pena. George had danced in the American Ballet Theatre, but he didn't know anything about figure skating. Debi had been having trouble landing her triple-triple. George said, "I want you to do the triple-triple, but right as you go into it, I want you to smile as if you were about to eat this thing alive." She did, and landed perfectly. Here's someone who knew nothing about figure skating but knew exactly what to say to Debi.

You can tell if you are going to miss a jump the split second before you go up. You have this feeling about whether your timing is right or not. Sometimes you can pull it off, even when you mess up, but usually you have this feeling right before you go, and you just know you are going to do it. It's really hard to explain, but it is an attitude. It's the way you are feeling about yourself.

You have to go in saying, "I'm going to go out there and *eat this thing alive.* I'm going to put everything into this because it's the greatest thing in the world." If you do, you'll get much better results. ■

"I always believe I can beat the best, achieve the best. I always see myself in the top position."

SERENA WILLIAMS,
*1999 Women's U.S. Open
tennis champion*

"No one ever said I would be any good or get to a Grand Slam final. In my teens, I wasn't expected to do anything. I've proved a lot of people wrong. I've tried so hard to do the best I can."

LINDSAY DAVENPORT,
*1998 Women's U.S. Open
tennis champion*

Chris EVERT

During Chris's first U.S. Open tennis championship, she and her mom were staying with her aunt and uncle in Larchmont, New York. On the first day, they went through the wrong gate at Forest Hills and had to walk about a mile. They didn't have a pass so they had to talk their way in. They spent most of the morning schlepping around the back courts, trying to figure out where the women's locker room was.

I have three victories that I cherish over the years. One of them was at the beginning of my career, one of them was in the middle, and one was at the end. The first was in 1969 when I was just fifteen years old and relatively unknown in tennis circles. I was a top junior, but I had never been exposed to any women's competition and this was a women's tournament in Charlotte, North Carolina.

I played Margaret Court, who had just won the Grand Slam. She was number one in the world, and I beat her 7–6, 7–6. Here I was, a total unknown, a child, coming out and beating the number one player. That win was full of fanfare. It was my introduction to fame and to the tennis world. People knew me from that moment on. It's always like that, the first time you have that big win. I was just this innocent fifteen-year-old little girl and couldn't believe all the commotion. I still remember that.

My second most memorable victory was against Tracy Austin at the 1980 U.S. Open in the semifinals. I had lost to her five times in a row. At that point Tracy was number one in the world, and there was no reason she shouldn't continue to dominate for the next ten years. I didn't think I would ever beat her again. I thought I was over the hill at twenty-five.

The day before I played Tracy I got some key advice from Pam Shriver's coach Don Candy. He said, "Chrissie, Tracy is a better offensive player than she is a defensive player, so you can't just play your normal counterpunching tennis with her and let her dictate the points. You have to step in from the first ball and be the aggressor. You have to be the attacking one. Take that away from her, put her on the defensive, and take chances, and, God forbid, take risks."

This style of play was uncharacteristic of me because I was a baseliner, but I did it. I was the aggressor in the first set and lost 6–4, but I remember feeling, Okay, I lost the first set, but I'm playing great so I've got to keep this up. I won the second set 6–1, and the third set 6–1. It was one of those midlife-career-crisis matches.

This match was pivotal, because if I had lost to her one more time I would have thought about retiring. I had been so depressed and yet I turned it around. I got some strength somewhere and played aggressively, and it was as if my victory was meant to be. That win rejuvenated me to play another ten years.

My third great memory is the 1985 French Open when I was thirty. Again, I'd lost ten straight times to

Martina Navratilova, and people were saying I would never beat her again. Martina was number one in the rankings and I was number two. I really didn't believe I could win the match, because after you've been drummed ten times in a row you don't have any confidence when you play that person. But I kept telling myself to hang in there, don't give up, forget about who I was playing and just play each point.

Throughout the entire match I was not confident of winning, but I wanted to stay with Martina to see what she would do. She came up with some pretty sloppy tennis shots at times, which made me realize she was nervous playing me too. I beat her in three sets in the finals, and again that match made me feel great about myself for the next three or four years. Just that one win alone.

Martina Navratilova and I are a big part of each other's careers, whether we like it or not. I think that Martina and I pushed each other to higher levels of our games. Because of her, I worked on my fitness. She was the first one to really come out and say it's not enough to practice hitting tennis balls. You need to do cross training and weights. It was because of Martina that I went to the gym and got stronger, and it was because of me that she learned patience and got mentally tougher and learned to have a better baseline game. We pushed each other mentally, physically, and also with respect to career longevity. If Martina hadn't come along, I might have been bored. ■

"There are certain times when you work, work, work, practice, practice, practice, and the physical part's there but emotionally something's happening in your life or mentally you're a little slack. It's very rare when all three— the physical, the mental, and the emotional—come together. I think what makes a champion is, when one thing's on but two things are off, you can still win the match."

CHRIS EVERT

"I wanted to win by playing well and hitting great shots. That's what I did. I didn't want to be out there just getting the ball back in. That's the mind-set I took. I was probably mentally more aggressive than in other matches. Hitting the winner at match point and hearing the roar of the crowd, that's something I'll never forget. It seriously was the greatest feeling you can experience as a professional athlete."

LINDSAY DAVENPORT,
upon winning the 1998 Women's U.S. Open tennis championship

Juli INKSTER

Juli was the story of 1999 on the LPGA tour. The thirty-nine-year-old mother of two enjoyed her best golf season ever. She won two major championships, the U.S. Open and the LPGA, a total of five tournaments, and nearly doubled her winnings from her previous most successful season, and surpassed $5 million in all-time earnings. Most importantly, she played her way into the LPGA Hall of Fame. As Juli said, "This is a year I will never forget."

Golf is not like baseball and tennis, where it's a reaction—you're there, you hit it, and boom! You have so much time to think in golf, it's hard to be positive all the time, and you're going to have those demons come in and try to take over.

The easiest thing to do when you're playing well is to have confidence. The hardest thing to do, because I've been there, is to play when you don't have confidence. You might hit it down the middle of the fairway and you're in a divot or you might hit it in the trees and you're behind a tree, but if you're playing well, it's weird; it seems like you have an open shot every time. The little things that go wrong when you're *not* playing well go right when you *are* playing well.

One of the ways I try to stay confident when my game isn't on is to keep in mind my three keys to success. One is to work hard. You've got to want something to achieve it. Two, you've got to be your own person. You've got to be a leader. You can't be a follower. You have to make your own decisions. And three, you've got to have a passion for what you're doing. ∎

"Success to me is getting married, having a family, teaching my children the way I was taught, and having my children believe in themselves."

BEA THOMAS,
After 64 years of coaching high school athletics in southern New Jersey

"You don't know what you can do, and with drugs you'll never find out. I believe in women. I believe in myself. I believe in my body. I believe I can run faster not using drugs than people can using drugs, because that's the way I was put here."

EVELYN ASHFORD,
1984 Olympic gold medalist in the 100-meter dash

"What makes a real winner is they believe in themselves, even though they might get burned at the stake for one lousy game, one lousy match, or one lousy slump. They are their own cheerleader and their own support system."

AIMEE MULLINS,
physically challenged sprinter

Aimee MULLINS

Aimee is a physically challenged sprinter, world record holder, and model. Avant-garde British designer Alexander McQueen used Aimee, with specifically carved prosthetic legs, as a runway model during London Fashion Week. He was accused of being a "voyeur-provocateur." McQueen answered, I wanted to show the beauty that comes from the inside." Aimee said, "I want to be seen as beautiful because of my disability, not in spite of it."

I was in blissful ignorance until about age eleven or twelve, because all the kids I knew grew up around me. I had never met another amputee until I was a teenager. I would make fun of myself and my wooden legs. I'd play the drums on them in the back of the bus. There was the shin part with the ankle and the socket, and then there's the foot part that was attached by a bolt. With substitute teachers I used to loosen the bolt and flip my foot around. It would really freak them out. When you showcase your disability first, it isn't a big deal. In fact, you can have fun with it. It's not a problem.

At puberty, though, every girl cares about what she looks like. But you get through that, especially if you realize everybody has some sort of a disability. Everybody wants to hide something they think is a detriment.

It's at that point, post puberty, that you figure out what oftentimes you thought made you the ugly duckling can really make you the swan, because it provides you with all the trials and tribulations that, if you face them head on, make you a strong person. It's enabling. It empowers you with something you wouldn't have otherwise. It's that moment of freedom when you forget about your loss and you can just have a good time.

I'm not going to lie and say I never went through times that weren't really difficult, but in all fairness I think it was not so much because of my legs as because of my age. I think everyone has some unpleasant memories of their early teens.

I'd love to do a fashion shoot. People ask me why the hell I would want to put myself into a world that is based on rejection and physical perfection. It's such a hard world to get into. But that's exactly why I want to get into it, because it needs to be shaken up.

When you open a fashion magazine, somebody is dictating what's beautiful. It's a very narrow spectrum. That's why so many young people are experiencing eating disorders after looking at images that have been manipulated. I believe we need an international symbol at the bottom of the page that shows the photo has been altered. If everybody who looks at it knows something on this photo was retouched, maybe they won't feel, Oh, my God, is that what a woman's body should look like?

I'm modeling to make a social statement, but I'm also doing it because it's fun. Look at someone with a pair of eyeglasses. It's no more of a prosthetic than my legs are. It's something you wear outside your body that functions as part of your body. But look at the fun people have designing eyewear.

I want to have fun like that with my legs. I think things can go beyond function, comfort, and performance. I'm taking the legs from the realm of being just an athletic apparatus to the realm of design, art, and fashion. I'd love to do a fashion shoot for a complete line of women's shoes, wearing a different pair of legs for each pair of shoes. ∎

> **"I'm really going into the lion's den
> with this fashion thing. I had my
> first shoot in New York City, and I
> was standing with these able-bodied
> models, when I felt some doubts
> start to creep into my head. I just sat
> down and thought, You're here
> because you deserve to be here. Yes!"**
> AIMEE MULLINS

> **"To me, beauty is when people
> radiate that they like themselves."**
> AIMEE MULLINS

"I just try to be me. I don't try to be like anybody else because when you do that, it kind of catches up with you. That's what my grandmother always taught me, to remain true to myself."

CHAMIQUE HOLDSCLAW,
winner of three NCAA basketball championships at Tennessee and number-one draft choice of the WNBA Mystics

"I've gotten a long way just on sheer optimism—taking jobs I was unqualified for, never believing I would fail at them, because I'm optimistic to the point of being naïve. I was willing to try things I probably should have failed at, and could have failed at, but didn't."

LIZ DOLAN,
president, Dolan St. Clair Sports Marketing

Liz DOLAN

Liz is a former Nike vice president and president of her own sports marketing company. One of the most valuable lessons Liz learned at Nike was Oregon track coach and Nike cofounder Bill Bowerman's philosophy: Winning is simply competitive response. A coach is a teacher of competitive response, because you never really know exactly what you have to do to win. You have to be able to look at the situation as you go along, and respond.

I ran the New York City Marathon twice. The first time I ran it in four hours and fifty minutes. My second time was four hours and fifty-nine minutes. So I retired. I was going the wrong way. I think of my two marathons as my first marathon and my last marathon.

The best team experience I ever had was the first marathon in 1993. I did it with four women friends. None of us had ever before done anything like it. We had been jogging together for a few years in the morning before work. The growth process with that group of women during the five months of training was an amazing experience for all of us. We went from really seriously thinking, This is impossible, to Oh, my God, we finished! I started to cry at the starting line, because I couldn't believe we were even

left: Jacqueline Gareau, Boulder, Colorado, November 1999

below: Nancy Lopez

left: Kristine Lilly
below: Gabrielle Reece

left: Melanie Benn.
November 10, 1999

below: Jean Driscoll, 1996

above: Silken Laumann
left: Juli Inkster

left: Katie Hnida, 1998

below: Aimee Mullins, 1996 Big East Outdoors

left: Joan Benoit Samuelson
below left: Michelle Kwan
below right: Serena Williams

above: Sylvie Bernier, Los Angeles, 1984
left: Chris Evert, 1985 French Open

above: Steffi Graf
left: Dawn Staley

left: Manon Rheaume

below: Amy Van Dyken

left: Lyn St. James
below: Shannon Miller

left: Julie Foudy

below: Rebecca Lobo

left: Mia Hamm

below: Picabo Street

left: Debi Thomas

below: Lindsey Davenport

left: Jennifer Capriati
below: Kerri Strug

left: Bonnie Blair
below: Marion Jones

left: Chamique Holdsclaw

below: The authors, Charlie Jones and
Kim Doren, with Inger Miller (center)

there, and I cried again at the finish line, because I couldn't believe we had all done it. It was just an amazing experience.

I'm not particularly athletic, so it was a mind game— tricking myself into *believing* I could run a marathon. Nothing has ever taught me more than that first marathon run, because if I can trick myself into believing I can run the New York City Marathon, I can trick myself into believing I can do anything. Why? Because there's no reason in the world why you should ever run a marathon! ■

"You will succeed if you believe it can be done; if you're willing to work hard while being smart about it; if you're willing to surround yourself with great people who will challenge you every day; if you're willing to take on the naysayers as a challenge, and if you're willing to strive for excellence while recognizing each day is an opportunity to learn."

AMY LOVE,

publisher and founder of
Amy Love's Real Sports *magazine*

Inger MILLER

Inger won the gold medal in the 200-meter and a silver medal in the 100-meter at the 1999 World Championships. Her father, Lennox, first coached her, and she said it worked because, "We didn't bring the track stuff home." Inger's career has been filled with tribulations, from a fractured navicular bone in her foot to flipping her car three times on the freeway just five weeks before the 1996 Olympic trials. A graduate of the University of Southern California, she ultimately plans to be a veterinarian.

Winning the gold medal in the 200-meter at the World Championships was my finest moment. It was one of those times when I knew I was going to win, but I also wanted to give a good showing. I wanted to run an exceptional time. I wanted to run a PR. When I got to the blocks I thought, Okay, let's just do it.

I came off the turn and had no idea where I was or where anybody was. I had tunnel vision. I was in my lane and all I could hear was my breathing. When I got to the finish line, I had to look around to make sure I was by myself. It felt so easy; it was almost as if I could have run another race. I had put everything together that I'd worked on.

The feeling I had doing it was incredible. I don't know how you can re-create it. It's one of those times when you go out and everything just clicks. Those are the best races you can have because it doesn't feel like you're working at all. It was one of those moments where it just *happened*. ■

"I'm not afraid of anybody. There is no pressure because whatever happens, happens, And there's nothing you can do about it. God controls everything, so I just go out on the track and have a good time."

INGER MILLER

Layne
BEACHLEY

Layne is a world champion surfer. She says it's really hard to express the spiritual nature of surfing. Only a surfer knows the feeling. It's an extremely natural high, but you never have complete satisfaction because once you do it, you want to do it again. You just want to keep doing it, over and over.

Self-belief happened when I stopped playing mind games with myself. You can be so superstitious that you play silly little games. For example, the girls I compete with are quite a tight unit because we all travel together and there are only a limited number of us. If I ever had to spend a day with them, I'd always try and stay one step ahead of them, because eventually it would prepare me to stay one step ahead of them in the heats.

It was just exhausting me. Instead of going out and believing I could win on the water, I had to play those silly games on land. Once again, it took my focus and my concentration away from what I should be doing, which is surfing and believing in my ability no matter what the conditions. Obviously, you have to train a lot, but basically it always comes down to believing in your own ability. ■

"Sometimes, in a world of
celebrities, we think these people
are like superheroes. But they're not.
They're just normal people who
have done great things. People will
say, 'Well, I could never be like that.'
But they can. There are so many
little girls who could grow up to
play on world championship teams."

CASSIE CAMPBELL,
Canadian hockey player

Cristen
POWELL

Cristen, at age nineteen, was the quickest woman in the world, with a top fuel drag run of 4.59 seconds. She loves drag racing and is addicted to speed. She just can't get enough of it. The fastest she's ever gone is 311 mph. While crunching her teeth and fighting all those G's, Cristen says it's unbelievable to go that fast.

The best advice I ever received was from my dad. It was more of a winning attitude he instilled in me. He used to always tell me, "There's nothing you can't do."

People say, "Wow, I can't believe you're a woman competing in this sport." And I say, "Why?" Because it's never been an issue for me. So what if I'm a female? I can do things just as good as any guy. I've never had the stereotypes other people have—that women can't do things as well as men. My dad gave me great values and taught me I could do anything I set my mind to, so I always have. ■

"Somehow, I find something every week to put me in contention. . . . I work hard, and confidence is a big thing, too. I really believe in myself, and I know what my ability is. I'm not happy with anything less than the best."

KARRIE WEBB,
*1999 LPGA Player of the Year
with six victories*

Ila
BORDERS

Ila is the first woman to pitch in a men's professional baseball game. Her first win was on July 24, 1998, and it really felt good because everybody said she couldn't do it. Ila's biggest thrill as a pitcher was winning the 1997 Northern League Championship. She pitched one inning in the playoffs, facing the number 2, 3, and 4 hitters, giving up no runs, and striking out the last batter. The hardest part was dealing with the media because they were always looking for a controversy. Ila says the men treated her very well, but the women didn't like her.

You've got to believe in yourself. It's not cockiness, but when you're out there on the mound you know the game revolves around you. You are it and everybody's counting on you, so you better get the job done.

Two things help me to be a winner. First, I try to stay on an even keel. I don't get too high and I don't get too low. Second, I do a lot of visualization. I never see a bad pitch. I always see a good pitch. Before every pitch I throw, I see where I want it to go; I've already thrown the ball in my mind, and it was a good pitch.

The more experience I have, the better I get and the more focused I am. Listening to loud music pumps me up, but as soon as I step on the mound, everything flies out the window and I'm just concentrating on throwing the ball where I want it to go. ■

"A lot of people think girls cannot do this. I want girls to see that they can."

FABIOLA DA SILVA,
best female in-line skater in the world

Sylvie BERNIER

Sylvie is a Canadian Olympic champion. She won the gold medal in springboard diving in 1984. Sylvie's dad always said, "Your sport is a hobby. Your school and your social life are even more important." So even if Sylvie was training thirty-five hours a week, she always tried to understand that equilibrium is more important than diving. "I think that saved me in a way," Sylvie says. "He made me realize that when I was very young, and it has always stayed with me."

Believing in yourself is everything. If you don't believe in what you can do, it's almost impossible to achieve it. You could have the best surroundings, you could have the best coach, you could have the best physiotherapist, you could have the best nutritionist, but if you don't believe in your capacity, if you don't believe you *deserve* to be the best in the world, you'll never make it to the top.

You don't have to be arrogant. I was very self-confident, but I never told anyone I wanted to win. I never said that. I always said, "I'll do my best." But deep inside I knew I wanted to win. If I was sitting down with my parents I would tell them, but I wouldn't tell my friends. I would just listen and say, I'm ready and I'll do what I can. But self-confidence is really *very* very important. ∎

"My mother taught me very early to believe I could achieve any accomplishment I wanted to. The first was to walk without braces."

WILMA RUDOLPH,
first American woman to win three track and field gold medals in a single Olympics

EIGHT

OVERCOME OBSTACLES

"I've learned you can overcome the biggest setbacks. I focus on turning negatives into positives. If you want it and you dream about it . . .there's nothing that's going to stop you."

CHRIS WITTY,
speed skater, the only U.S. Olympic double medalist at Nagano in 1998

Silken
LAUMANN

One of the most dramatic stories in Olympic history belongs to Canadian rower Silken Laumann, the 1992 Barcelona gold medal favorite in single sculls. Ten weeks before the Games she was on the water warming up for a regatta in Essen, Germany, when a men's pair rammed her wooden boat. Their splashboard drove right into her leg. Silken said, "It was like being cut with two hundred knives, and when I looked down my muscle was hanging at my ankle and I could see my bone."

Remarkably, after weeks in the hospital and seven separate surgeries, she was not only able to return as a competitor, she won the bronze medal.

I'm a very determined person. When I decide I want something, I'm very single-minded. I had trained a long time for the opportunity to win an Olympic gold medal, and I had already been through so much. I started rowing in 1983, so I took almost ten years to be in the position to win. The last three years before the 1992 Olympics, I had a wonderful series of successes and my confidence was high. I was really enjoying the sport, but more than anything, I was focused on achieving my goals and fulfilling my potential.

When this obstacle came up, I suddenly had a doctor in Germany telling me, "Your Olympics are over. You'll be able to row again, recreationally, and hopefully you'll be able to walk without too much of a limp." Part of my brain just couldn't accept it was over. I'm thinking, What do you mean? I've been training for this for ten years. It *can't* be over. It was fortunate that I had that mind-set. There were a few days after the accident when I was really discouraged and in shock, and I just couldn't believe it had happened. I honestly didn't think it was possible I would go to the Olympics. The whole time I was recovering, there was only a part of me that truly believed I'd go to the Olympics again. But more than anything, I just had to get back into the boat as soon as possible. I had to feel "normal" again. And rowing is what was normal for me. That's what I *did*. The injury was so massive and depressing that if I had embraced reality, it would have overwhelmed me. So I didn't embrace it; just denied it. And denial was good.

I was in the hospital twenty-three days. When I first got back in the boat, it felt like I had come home. It felt great even though I couldn't stand without pain. When I would stand up, my whole leg would turn bright purple from the circulation damage. I really couldn't do anything without pain. I couldn't make my own meals; I couldn't walk across the room. Nothing. But I could row. It was bizarre. Part of the reason was that in rowing your legs are out in front of you, you're not standing, so I didn't have the same circulation problem. On land I could barely walk. I was uncomfortable. I had to sit down all the time, and I felt so inactive and so unlike myself. But when I got into the boat, even though it wasn't as good as it was before, it felt normal. I felt normal. I was revitalized by it, and seven weeks after leaving the hospital I was able to finish third in single sculls in Barcelona.

My Olympic bronze medal was unlike any other medal I've won. In a funny way, I felt a huge amount of relief because it had been such a struggle and I was so unbelievably tired, not just from the race but from the entire effort. The first moment I allowed myself to really feel it was after the race. What I intellectualized about the experience was that it was such a wonderful example of how, if you don't allow your mind to create barriers and limits for yourself, anything is possible. It was wonderful. The whole grandstand was cheering for me and I had so much support and love around me. All my friends and family were there. It was an experience unlike anything I've ever had before. An amazing feeling of family. Not only my friends and family but the entire country. ■

Lyn
ST. JAMES

Lyn is the second woman and the oldest rookie ever to qualify for the Indy 500. She was named 1992 Rookie of the Year. Lyn calls auto racing the most challenging of all sports because it requires 100 percent mental concentration and 100 percent physical energy at the same time. There's no football huddle, tennis changeover, or basketball time-out to relax and gather your thoughts. Throughout the entire race you're working hard physically and, at the same time, you're challenged mentally.

Race car drivers are not just born, it's a trained skill. When you sit in a race car your physical space is the parameters of that car. You literally wear the car; the car becomes part of you. It's like putting on your clothes; you feel everything. You feel every pebble you drive over, every movement in the suspension, every heartbeat of the engine. You meld and become one with the car.

I was not real good in the beginning, but I probably wasn't as bad as I was afraid I was going to be. I worked harder at it than most anybody I know. I was determined. I loved it. It was very challenging.

However, in 1986 in Riverside, I was involved in a crash that destroyed three race cars. I didn't cause it; someone else did. I was driving for the Ford Motor Company, and it was relatively early in my career. I was extremely worried. I got hurt, not badly, but I demolished a million dollars' worth of equipment. I hurt physically, but mentally I was destroyed. I was scared to death this was going to be the end of my career.

But as it turned out, it actually became a positive part of my career. Top executives at the Ford Motor Company said, "Whoa, she really is running with the big boys!" In other words I earned their respect, because the first time they saw me involved in a crash, I didn't cry and I didn't want to give up. I didn't do some of the things they expected a woman to do.

That experience made me a better driver because I had never had a really bad crash before, and this was a really bad crash and I walked away. My gear worked, my suit and helmet were singed, but I didn't get burned anywhere. Somehow, when you stand there and see debris all around you and realize you've just walked away, you know your stuff works. So something deep inside me made me a better driver after that, which actually impressed other people. They felt more confidence in me. But when you're standing amongst the wreckage, that isn't what you're thinking about. You're wondering if this is the end of your career. ■

Picabo STREET

Picabo is a member of the U.S. national ski team and is an Olympic gold and silver medalist. Picabo says the coolest, most special part of winning her Olympic gold medal was the fact that it was so unexpected. The event was the super-G, but her specialty was the downhill. To keep them separated, Picabo has names for all of her skis. Her downhill skis are called "Arnolds," and it was on a pair of "Arnolds" that she won the super-G.

In 1990, when I was dropped from the U.S. ski team, I cut my own throat. I stuck my neck out and created obstacles for myself. I was testing everybody with, "Let me see how nasty an attitude I can show up with at camp, because I don't know if I really want to be here at age fifteen, and I don't like having somebody tell me what to do with my life. Especially now that my parents live in Hawaii and I live by myself. Let me test the system."

I was lost. I was rebelling. I didn't know if I wanted to be so regimented and have someone tell me how to train and what to eat every day. I like to make those decisions for myself. But it wasn't about making decisions. It was about the discipline, the structure, the control of someone else telling me what to do.

I always squirmed in those situations. In order to return to the team, I had to figure out how to make this situation work for me—how I could conform and be part of it, and still find some way in which I didn't have to completely give up control. I'd still have some, but I'd have it within team boundaries. ∎

"When someone tells me there is only one way to do things, it always lights a fire under my butt. My instinct is, 'I'm going to prove you wrong.'"

PICABO STREET

Chris EVERT

Chris's international tennis ranking was never lower than number four in all nineteen years of her professional career. Her battles with Martina Navratilova raised the level of women's tennis to dizzying heights. Chris's consistent ground strokes and strong baseline game were matched against Martina's more aggressive style. They faced each other in a total of fourteen Grand Slam finals. Although Martina won more of the matches (ten to four), Chris won the first in 1975 and the last in 1986. Both finished their careers with eighteen Grand Slam titles.

My toughest defeat was in the 1984 U.S. Open finals against Martina Navratilova. I won the first set 6–4 and got a standing ovation from 18,000 people. This was when Martina was ranked number one. I was playing *really* well, and I was completely into it. Then I lost the second set 6–4 and the third 6–4.

I remember going up to the net and shaking hands, but I just couldn't bring myself to say anything. I couldn't say, "Nice match." I couldn't say, "You played great." I couldn't put my arms around her. I wasn't mad, I was devastated. I just wanted to burst into tears. The presentation was really tough because I felt like I played the best I could and I still couldn't beat her.

I gave myself a week off to recover. I went home to Fort Lauderdale. I regrouped. I went to the beach. I was always good at living in the present. If I won a huge tournament, two weeks later I'd forget it; I wouldn't think about it. I'd think about what I was doing at that point. So nothing really stayed with me for months on end.

You have to understand that the mental part of the game is where my strength was. I was a very good athlete, but not an exceptional one like Martina or Steffi. I was exceptional mentally. I had the ability to concentrate 100 percent on every point and stay *in the now* and not be distracted. It's good and it's bad. It's good in tennis and it's bad in life. There could be wars all over the world and I would be, "Yeah, but I won 6–4 in the third." ■

"When I play, I'm boiling inside. I just try not to show it because it's a lack of composure, and if you give in to your emotions after one loss, you're liable to have three or four losses in a row."

CHRIS EVERT

Andrea
JAEGER

As a teenage player, Andrea was ranked as high as number two in the world before an injury ended her tennis career. Her most memorable victory was beating Billie Jean King in the semifinals at Wimbledon. Andrea was eighteen, and she just thought it would be a great experience to go against Billie Jean. It was. Andrea played the best match of her life and won 6–1, 6–1. As they were leaving the court, Billie Jean paused, turned around, and took a long look back. This was the last singles match she would ever play on Centre Court at Wimbledon.

My whole world when I was young was the Olympics. I grew up watching Nadia Comaneci and Olga Korbut in gymnastics and seeing all those other sports, and I thought that was the coolest thing in the world. But tennis was never part of the Olympic Games, so it never entered my mind as a long-range goal.

Then in 1984, in Los Angeles, tennis became a demonstration sport in the Olympics and I was seeded number one. I had injured my shoulder at the French Open in May so I didn't play Wimbledon, hoping I could play in Los Angeles, because the Olympics was the greatest event you could ever participate in.

I went to Los Angeles and my shoulder was still bad. I failed my physical, and the doctors said, "You shouldn't be competing, but let's see how it goes. We're going to have to play it by ear." I won my first match, but I literally couldn't even get dressed the next morning. It hurt just to put my shirt on. I couldn't lift my arm. I couldn't open a car door. So they had to default me in the second round.

I was so bummed. My whole country was supporting me, and I was defaulting after being seeded number one. That was the only time I was ever really upset about anything in tennis. I went back to my room and I just cried. My teammates and my coach brought me a gigantic chocolate chip cookie, and I just sat and ate the chocolate chip cookie and cried all night.

I grew up being really strong, so the next day when the reporters said, "You don't look like you're upset," I replied, "No. I am, but you can't tell." I always had to present myself as tougher than what the situation was. I also knew that because I defaulted I took a place from somebody else who could have had the opportunity to play in the Olympics. I still feel really bad about that. It took me a long time to recover—two phases of the Summer Olympics before I could even watch it on television. ∎

"I learned very early that life is not about being a superstar athlete. You can't let stardom be your existence because, if you do, you will fail every time."

ANDREA JAEGER

Jean DRISCOLL

Jean won the Boston Marathon seven consecutive times in the women's wheelchair division. She says her first victory in 1990 was very special because she didn't think she belonged in the race. Her coach, Marty Morse, coerced her after she won a 12K in Spokane, Washington. Jean didn't think she was prepared for the hills, but she was. She ended up winning and breaking the record by almost seven minutes.

The 1998 Boston Marathon was probably my biggest surprise in racing, my biggest upset in racing, and my biggest disappointment in racing. It's hard to put into a concise little word package what that race was all about.

What happened was I got away from Louise Sauvage. She's an Australian and my main competitor. I was in great shape, and my bread and butter has always been the hills, and sure enough there's this hill at mile 17. You take a right-hand turn and immediately you start climbing. It is the steepest hill on the Boston Marathon course. Heartbreak Hill is the longest, but this hill by the firehouse is the steepest, and more times than not I have gotten away from my competition there.

I made the right-hand turn at mile 17. I started digging in, climbing as hard as I could. My strategy worked again and I got away from Louise. Every hill I got a little bit farther and farther ahead of her, but then I came to Cleveland Circle, which is at the 22-mile mark. You make a right-hand turn and go down the hill. There are trolley tracks in the left-hand lane. You make a sweeping left turn and head toward Boston and the finish line.

In 1997, I had a wheel slip into the trolley track and I crashed. It's the first Boston I didn't win. So this time, as I went through Cleveland Circle, I was very tentative, very cautious. I must have put my brake on three different times. I slowed down to go over the trolley tracks, and when I had successfully negotiated them I waved to the crowd—they were going crazy, because they knew what had happened the year before—and kept going.

Louise went full bore through that section and made up most of what I had gained on her on the hills. I could tell she had closed on me, but I didn't know by how much. On the Boston course, your last turn is a left-hand turn, and then you have about 500 meters to the finish line. When I turned left, I saw Louise was only about 50 meters behind me and I thought, A 50-meter lead should be enough to hold her off. So I just put my head down and pushed as hard as I could down toward the finish line. It seems like that last 500 meters takes forever. You're so tired, and the finish line just keeps slipping farther and farther back. As I got within 15 feet of it I heard the finish line announcer saying, "Jean Driscoll, eight-time winner of the Boston Marathon," and I took my last stroke, raised my arms to cut the tape—and Louise cut it.

I was thinking, What happened? I was numb. I couldn't believe it. I thought I had her by 20 or 30 meters. The crowd was so excited and so into it, and all of a sudden you could have heard a pin drop. At the finish line of the Boston Marathon there are millions of people, and they all went silent.

It was amazing. This rush of numbness overcame me and I stopped. What happened? Oh, my gosh, I had this race won. *What happened?* People were running up to me asking if I was okay. I was, like, Yeah, yeah. I could hardly get words together, and then after maybe a minute or so, Louise came back, and she was so psyched she was hugging me. Then she went up to get her laurel wreath and I went down toward the cameras and started doing interviews.

I don't even remember a whole lot about the questions. I just remember being flooded with cameras and reporters asking questions about what happened and I was still trying to figure it out. Then they called me back to the victory stand area. The second-place person is never asked to go back, but Louise and I finished so close they gave us the same time—1:41:19. I returned to the area and Larry Rawson from ESPN was doing the interview, which was amplified so all the people in the stands could hear it. I don't even remember the questions Larry asked. I just remember saying, "Louise is awesome. For her to come from behind like that—she's just awesome."

It took about a day for everything to sink in, but Tuesday morning when I woke up my heart hurt so bad. Tuesday was probably my hardest day to get through, because that's when it started to hit me. But one of the nice things that came out of that marathon was I realized people are not only interested in the winner, they're also interested in the character of others who are in the race.

I know I am somebody whom people look up to, and people watch me very closely, but I don't think about that stuff on race day. Let's face it, it's so easy to be happy and to share the excitement with everybody when you win. But the neat thing was the media, reporting on how gracious I was when I was not feeling gracious at all. I don't know what was coming out of my mouth, but everybody—both print and electronic media people—everybody gave me such good press it was overwhelming.

This really touched my heart, because deep down the character I have is what came through and that's what people saw, even though I wasn't feeling it. I have a very strong Christian faith and I think God was just carrying me along, because I honestly couldn't figure things out until days after the race. It was one of the most heart-hitting experiences I've ever faced. ■

"A winner's strongest muscle is her heart."

CASSIE CAMPBELL,
gold medalist for Team Canada at the 1994 and 1997 Women's World Hockey Championships

Jean
DRISCOLL

Jean was named 1991 Women's Sports Foundation Amateur Sportswoman of the Year. For Jean, success is being committed and then going out and doing everything she can. Jean wants to leave it all out there on the course. Based on her training and her level of commitment, if she meets those goals, then she's successful. Jean is the five-time winner of the George Huff Award for athletic and academic excellence at the University of Illinois.

I really want to help people understand how I view my wheelchair. Lots of times people pass somebody in a wheelchair on the street and they'll think, Oh, my gosh, I don't know how they do it. Lots of people can't even look at me. You just want to shake them and say, I'm doing fine. I'm probably doing better than you are.

The way I view my wheelchair is like a pair of eyeglasses. First thing in the morning, people put on their glasses and forget about them for the rest of the day. They don't go through the day thinking, Oh, another day of nearsightedness. What am I going to do? The same is true with my chair. It's the first thing I look for in the morning, but I don't think about it during the day. I forget I'm using it. My life has so many other interests. I'd love for people to see that's where my focus is; it's not on the fact that I'm sitting down.

When people first started engaging in sports in their wheelchairs, people thought, Well, isn't that nice but really should they be out there? They're so fragile, and what happens if they fall out of their wheelchairs, for heaven's sake? Now that attitude is changing. The disability is secondary. It's a characteristic. I think that because attitudes are changing we're moving in the right direction. We're not there yet, but we're moving in the right direction. ∎

"I love my life. I'd rather be me."

JEAN DRISCOLL

Dawn
STALEY

Dawn was raised in a North Philadelphia housing project. It was not the greatest environment in the world, but Dawn took the positiveness of what people had to offer and ran with it. She is forever in debt to the people of her neighborhood who looked out for her. Dawn went on to become an outstanding basketball player at the University of Virginia, in the Olympic Games, and in the WNBA.

My toughest loss was in 1991. Tennessee beat Virginia in the National Championship game. We knew they were going to be tough, but we went into the game feeling pretty good. We were prepared. It was crazy, because the game went into overtime. I had the ball in my hand with six seconds left and the score was tied. I was coming up the court full steam ahead. I was thinking, as I was going in for the layup, that I was behind all the defenders. I thought I was, anyway.

So I took my two steps to make the layup, and while I'm taking these two steps I'm thinking how I'm going to react when I make it. I couldn't believe how easy it had been to get by them. The game was on the line. I thought it was a piece of cake. So on my way to the basket I was taking my two steps, thinking, Oh, my God, how am I going to react after I make this basket? That was what was going through my head.

I went in for the left-handed layup and it got blocked. I couldn't believe it. That wasn't in my plan, two seconds before I shot it. But I missed it, I missed the shot. Tennessee came back and scored. They tied the game and we went into overtime, and they went on to win.

I couldn't even cry. I truly thought we gave 110 percent. Perhaps that particular victory just wasn't meant to be. It was crazy, because we should have won that game. We were up by four with 1:20 left. The loss was really hard to accept, but what made me feel okay was knowing I had another year left in college, and we had an opportunity to try again. ∎

Annie
MEYERS
DRYSDALE

After playing for UCLA's women's national championship basketball team, where she became the first four-time All-American of either sex, and winning a silver medal in the Olympics, Annie became the first woman ever to sign with an NBA team. She is a television broadcaster for the WNBA, a member of the Basketball Hall of Fame, and the mother of three.

It was as big a shock to me as it was to everybody else when I was offered a tryout with the Indiana Pacers in the NBA. The challenge was second nature to me. I've played against guys all my life, so what I was doing was nothing different. I had been to the Olympics, I'd won a silver medal, and I'd received my degree at UCLA. The Pacers offered me a personal contract. I was not drafted, I was signed as a free agent with a one-year deal for $50,000. Where was a woman graduating from college going to make that kind of money in 1979? It was the opportunity of a lifetime, which most men never get.

Another motivating factor in trying out had to do with high school memories of wanting to try out for the boys' team. I really wanted to play on the boys' team during the school year because that's where the competition was, but a lot of people had talked me out of it by saying, "You're going to get hurt, you won't get to play, you're a girl." I was really intimidated so I didn't try out.

That event taught me that I don't want to look back on my life and say, "What if?" That's something I tell kids. Don't worry about failure. Try it, and if it doesn't work out that's okay, because at least you tried. Don't say *would of, should of, could of,* or *what if I'd done that?* You have to learn how to lose and learn how to win at the same time.

My goal was to try out as a ballplayer and make the team. I believed in my ability because I'd been playing basketball my whole life. There were some things I didn't do as well as the men, but there were other things I did as well as a lot of them. The assistant coach told me my fundamentals were better than half of the guys out there.

I had great teachers along the way, and I think I really had a knack for understanding the game. I was blessed with a lot of instincts about what needed to be done on the court. Now physically whether I could have gotten it done or not is still a question, but believe me, I was willing to become the eleventh man. I told them I could sit on the bench as well as some of those other guys, and I'd look a lot better in a uniform than most of them.

Physically and mentally I was the best prepared I had ever been to play the game of basketball. We went through the three-day tryout, and I performed as well as I could. I know I did my best. I was disappointed that the coach didn't keep me on the team at least through the preseason, because I believed I had all the qualifications they expect from the free agents and rookies who go to the next level. But he didn't feel that way. He never said I didn't make the team, but in our conversation after the last practice I knew I was not a member of the Pacers as a basketball player.

However, as disappointed as I was, signing a personal service contract was the opening of a new career in announcing. We had stipulated that I would broadcast for the Pacers if I didn't make the team. But I wasn't ready to give up playing, and in a couple of months I got my release so I could sign on the WBL and play for the New Jersey Gems. ■

"You can never meet everyone's expectations. It's hard enough to meet your own."

ANDREA JAEGER,
winner of her first pro tennis tournament
at age fourteen

Sheila
CORNELL-
DOUTY

Sheila was the first baseman on the U.S. national softball team that won the gold medal in the 1996 Olympics. She is proud of the three teenage children of her future husband, who were her cheering section and training partners. They wouldn't let her skip a practice. Sheila thought it was cool that she had three teenagers at the Olympics who wouldn't sell their gold medal game tickets for five hundred dollars. They said, "There's no way we'll scalp our tickets. We're here for you."

I think of part of my collegiate career as a failure. I went from being the top athlete in my high school to UCLA, where I expected to be a starter my freshman year. The girl who played first base was a senior, but I had played on teams with her in the past and I had always started. Now she was the starter. This was the first time I had to deal with that situation.

The biggest thing I did was to try to work as hard as I could in practice and to make sure I didn't talk negatively around my teammates. Softball is a team sport. I'm very much into the team, and the team we had at UCLA was really close. It was just like family. I tried to make sure my feelings didn't ever affect us on the field. One thing that helped me: I was friends with the girl who played first base.

I would never say, "Oh, it's okay to play in front of me, because I like you even though I think I play better." But in some ways being friends made it a little bit easier to deal with.

Part of my biggest failure, however, had to do with the mental side of the game. It took me a couple of years at UCLA before I overcame my mental obstacles. I struggled because I put so much pressure on myself when I did get opportunities that it was frustrating. I think in many ways dealing with my college situation was a really good learning experience. It made me a lot stronger ballplayer down the road.

My teammates say I'm the best mental player in the game because of how I'm able to focus and concentrate. A lot of that is due to those two years of struggling at UCLA. ■

"I try to have a positive attitude when life throws a curve. It's all relative. I have been so lucky in my life that I try to never feel sorry for myself."

MIA HAMM,
three-time ACC Player
of the Year in soccer

Melanie BENN

I was a freshman at Humboldt State, and I had come home to San Diego for the holidays. I got very sick on Christmas Eve with what I thought was the flu. I went to bed early, getting progressively sicker as the night went on. I noticed some red dots on my hands and my stomach. It worsened and the dots turned blue. I went to the emergency room, but I wasn't diagnosed for a couple of days. I only remember about an hour of being there. The next thing I knew it was Valentine's Day.

I was pretty much out of it for about six weeks. During that

On Christmas Day in 1995, nineteen-year-old Melanie came down with flulike symptoms that turned out to be a rare form of spinal meningitis. The disease necessitated the immediate amputation of all four limbs, and she spent the next few months fighting for her life. Almost two years later, Melanie was watching the San Diego Triathlon Challenge, and became inspired to be a participating athlete rather than a spectator. The next year, she completed the 1.2-mile rough water swim as a relay team member. Melanie was honored later that day with the 1998 Most Inspirational Athlete Award, presented by her favorite movie star, Robin Williams.

time I had been diagnosed with meningicaucus. They treated it, but the lasting effects from this blood disease had damaged my extremities so I didn't have circulation in my hands or feet. My arms had to be amputated below the elbows and my legs were amputated above the knees. I needed tons and tons of skin grafting, so I was in the burn unit at UCSD Medical Center for two months while they did about fifteen surgeries.

I was unconscious for most of it, but I had an amazing amount of support from my family and my friends. I constantly had people with me and nobody ever let me get down. I was sad, obviously, but I wasn't allowed to sit by myself and think about it. I was constantly being stimulated while I was in the hospital, and that helped a lot.

A little over a year later I saw the Triathlon Challenge and it changed my life. I decided that was what I wanted to do, and that's where I met my swimming coach, Alan Voisard. I've always loved swimming. I found I could still do it. It was good exercise, and it got me back into sports.

I showed up at Alan's practice, and he asked if I needed a lift to get in the pool. I said no and jumped in, and we started swimming, so it was cool. I worked with him all year and built up my strength and my skills. I have paddles that I use for my arms. They strap on the end of my residual limbs. (This is the politically correct term. You aren't supposed to say "stumps" anymore.) They're just like paddles. When I do my upstroke out of the water they have flexible hinges on them so they bend, and when I do my downstroke they offer some displacement in the water. It's pretty simple.

I have prostheses for my legs, but I don't use them for swimming. I prefer to be as unrestricted as possible in the water, because it's very freeing for me to be able to get out of my wheelchair and to move around as much as I can. When I'm walking I have my prosthetics on and it's kind of limiting; it is also limiting when I'm in my wheelchair. But in the water I'm on the same level as everyone else. I like being able to swim and to be alone with my thoughts.

Next, I decided to train for the La Jolla Rough Water Swim. Alan and I went out a couple of Saturday mornings and swam the mile-long ocean course. I had to overcome my fear of the ocean. It was scary being out there, but once you get in the water it's pretty good. I came in next to last out of thirty-five women in my age group. I was just glad I didn't have to get dragged back in to shore. I really enjoyed the competition.

My next event was the Triathlon Challenge. I was on a relay team with Mary Thompson, who did the bike part. She's a quadriplegic. I did the swim portion, which is about 1.2 miles. We also had a celebrity on our relay, Alexandra Paul, who did the run. She's an actress on *Baywatch*. We weren't really out there to win, but we did well. We finished and, most important, we had a good time. It was a great event. ■

**"Balance the good with the bad. Be
able to be happy when you're happy,
and sad when you're sad, and be
okay with both of them."**

MELANIE BENN

Chris

WITTY

Chris's goal is to win an Olympic gold medal in speed skating and an Olympic medal in cycling. She's finding out just how difficult it is to achieve her new goals. "It's tough to try to balance both sports because you never get a break, going right from one to the other," she says. Chris knows it would be easier to just forget it. But she doesn't want to limit herself. "I think I'm capable of being good in both sports," she adds. "Even if it gives me gray hair."

The finals of the 1000-meter race at Nagano was very stressful. The whole day was hard; there was more pressure on that race than any other race I'd ever been in. Being the record holder in the 1000 and getting a bronze medal in the 1500-meter added pressure. Instead of thinking about what I needed to do to skate a good race and focusing on that, my mind was headed in the wrong direction. On the day of the race, there were a lot of cameras in my face and things I wasn't used to, which added tons more pressure. When I went to the start line, I'd definitely never been that nervous before in my entire life. The moment had come, and now I had to do it. That's what I trained for.

Before the start I was sort of paying attention to the other times and the other skaters to see what they were doing. I always pay attention to times, because the best skaters go last. As the races went on, the times got faster and faster. I was in the last pair, so I knew what time I had to skate. In a way this made me even more excited, because the time was not that fast, and I knew I could beat it. This just added to my stress at the start line, and I false-started. So we had to go back to the start line again.

The person I was paired with was a Canadian with two silver medals in the 500. Her first 600 meters were always great, but her last lap was usually not that strong. So I thought, if I could just stay with her for 600 meters, on my last lap I'd have so much speed going I'd easily win. I ended up rushing a little bit, getting ahead of myself because I tried to chase her instead of focusing on my race.

At that moment I was so worked up from all the other things going on that I did what I shouldn't have done: I thought about the race. Normally, when you have a good race, you're not thinking, you're just doing. I was thinking and I came in second, just missing the gold.

At first it was heartbreaking to see I was so close and could have won if I'd skated my normal race. It was my toughest defeat. Nonetheless, you try to make it positive somehow. I took that race and said, "I did this right, I did this wrong," and I learned from it. The next time I'll know what to expect from being a medal favorite: how much pressure it is and what all the distractions are. I'll remember and try to put what I learned toward winning my next Olympic event. ■

"I can be a graceful loser, but I still take it really hard. I ask what I did wrong, and I focus on turning the negatives into positives. That's how you become successful."

CHRIS WITTY

"You face adversity all the time. I accept what lies ahead and then I do my best. You can't take things too seriously, and you can't use things as an excuse, or you'll never get through."

KRISTINE LILLY,
*winner of the Hermann Trophy,
college soccer's highest honor*

"You have to remember that no matter how big your goals or how many you have, there are going to be times when you miss by a little bit. You have to be realistic and flexible. One reason I have so many smaller goals is that even if my big goals don't happen, I've still achieved so much along the way, I don't feel the loss."

SHANNON MILLER,

Most decorated gymnast in U.S. history, with seven Olympic and nine World Championship medals

Kelly MOORE

Kelly is a champion windsurfer, who was the best in the world for a long time. But it was also a long time before she had the confidence to be a world champion. The one thing that might hold her back from winning in the future is that she is realizing just how important other things in her life have become.

The Aloha Classic was the final event of the 1998 season, and I was going into it in third place. This was for the world championship. I had the chance to move up or become world champion, depending on how I did in comparison with the two girls who were ahead of me. Since it was on Maui, my home surf, everyone was expecting me to do well, and so was I. This was the first contest where I really felt confident. It was the first time I was ready to win and knew I was going to win. I was floating on air. I was talking to myself on the water, just saying, "You know what, I'm ripping." It was unbelievable. I was a different person.

I was winning. I won all my heats. However, because the weather conditions were kind of sketchy, the race director was afraid we might not be able to finish. He wanted at least to get a men's result so the sponsors would be happy. He kept pushing the women back and instead of feeding in a women's heat after a certain number of men's rounds, he kept the women on hold and ran all the men's heats.

Then, when it finally came time for us, two of the guys who were in the semifinals went out by mistake. They thought it was their heat. Instead of calling them back in and sending us out, he released the women for the day and let the men continue. If things had been run properly, we would have finished.

When it came down to the very last day, they had a men's result, but they didn't start the women's competition until about one-thirty in the afternoon. I had been out there for a solid hour in conditions that were totally sailable, totally contestable, and the race director just putzed around and started the heats too late.

We ran my heat and I was winning, but the wind shut off one heat before we had an official result. I had already won, because the two girls in front of me had gotten knocked out in the first and second rounds so I was way ahead of them on points. But they didn't finish the heat after mine, so there was no valid result for the event that would have made me world champion.

It's 100 percent the fault of our own Professional Windsurfers Association, which is pretty sad. That was it. The decision was made. All the girls came to the beach, asking why they canceled the heat after mine. It was almost as if there was some agenda. Everyone was shocked. Even the guys, who are normally chauvinistic, were saying they were really sorry. But that's what happened.

And how did I handle it? Well, I didn't want to get out of bed for about a week. I wasn't feeling sorry for myself. It wasn't that. It was just too much to take. I wanted to be alone. I didn't want to talk to anyone. I didn't want to hear about it. They were trying to interview me, and I would say three words and burst into tears. I was completely devastated. Everything I'd worked for and trained for and sacrificed for up until that moment was in my hands. I had been floating on air, knowing I didn't even have to win another heat. I didn't even have to go out and sail. I was world champion—and then the next thing you know, *boom!* The wind dies fifteen minutes short of completing the event.

I just kept telling myself that everything happens for a reason, and I know there are more important things in life, but when you come that close and it's just ripped away from you, it's hard. It was totally avoidable. That's what made it so devastating. It was a blatant disregard for women. It was discrimination. It was unacceptable on the part of our association.

I'm surrounding myself with good true friends, people who keep me positive and are very supportive and understand what I'm going through. They don't try to make me feel better; they just let me work through it. Yes, I'm coming back. I'm not going to let them shoot me down. It's all part of being tough and bouncing back. I'll be sailing at sunset tonight. It'll be absolutely gorgeous, as long as I don't get stuck out there, because as I found out, the winds can die on you. ■

Cassie
CAMPBELL

Cassie plays for the Canadian national hockey team, the 1994 and 1997 Women's World Champions, and was named to the 1997 Directorate All-Star team. Cassie has an honors sociology degree from the University of Guelph and in 1996 was named their sportswoman of the year. However, Cassie and her Canadian teammates had a disappointing Olympic trip to Japan.

We were the favorites in women's ice hockey at the 1998 Olympics in Nagano. We had already won all the world championships before that, so to lose to the United States team, obviously our biggest rivals, was a devastating experience. At the same time, it was probably one of the best experiences of my life, because I got the chance to go to the Winter Olympics, and it was the first time female hockey players could go. Nonetheless, that loss was so disappointing I took a long time to get over it, and sometimes I don't think I'm there yet. I use it to motivate me in future endeavors and future games, and it's really the driving force behind why I'm still training and still playing.

You replay the mistakes you make on the ice over and over. You ask yourself, What should I have done? But basically, you just have to take that loss and learn from it and turn it back into a positive experience. ∎

"You're not human if you don't have self-doubts. I think self-doubts are a way for God, or whoever you may believe in, to make sure we're taking care of ourselves, and asking questions about ourselves. Am I where I want to be? Is this what I really want to do? Can I do this? I think self-doubts are just an extra challenge that is given to us so we can become the best person we can be."

CASSIE CAMPBELL

Leonore McDANIELS

Leonore first heard of the Virginia State Senior Olympic Games when she was fifty-nine years old. She thought it would be a lot of fun, so she and her husband signed up for tennis. When they learned there were some off days, Leonore also signed up for the 100-meter and the long jump to fill the time. She won both events and took off, running, jumping, and pole vaulting. At age seventy, she set four track and field records for her age group. Leonore was voted 1998 Top Female Masters Performer by USA Track & Field.

At the Nike World Masters Games I signed up for ten events because we had to stay for two weeks, and I didn't want to get bored. I didn't get to do all of them because of some time conflicts. I had set a personal goal in the pole vault of seven feet at seventy years of age. I figured that was a good number. And I cleared 7 feet 1 inch, setting a brand-new world record in the pole vault. I had been trying for a year and a half, and finally in Eugene, Oregon, it happened. I was really thrilled.

It was exceedingly hot that week and everybody was very tired by the time we started the 300 hurdles. I misjudged one and knocked it down, and it knocked me down and I fell on my hand and my body fell on top of my wrist.

I broke something, although I didn't know it at the time. I just rolled over, got up, and went on, but later I noticed something was wrong so I went to the first-aid people. They ended up putting a cast on my arm, right when I was supposed to be running the 200-meter.

I still had the long jump, the triple jump, and the 80-meter hurdles remaining. But everybody advised me not to run the hurdles with the cast on because it would pull me off balance. So I competed in the two field events. They wrapped my arm with plastic to keep sand out of the cast, and it worked. I exceeded the American record in both the long jump and in the triple jump, and I won a total of five gold medals. ■

"I have respect and admiration for our great women sports stars, because I can identify with the determination and dedication it takes to strive to do your very best. The goal to win, and the road leading to it, is laced with ups and downs, disappointments and ecstasies."

LEONORE
MCDANIELS

Lisa RAINSBERGER

Lisa, who has won marathons all over the world, started out as a swimmer. She set an age-group world record when she was only ten years old. She seldom lost, but on one occasion when she did, she cried. "I had to learn how to deal with disappointment," she says. "I haven't yet learned how to deal with failure because I don't consider myself a failure."

I started running between seasons to stay fit for swimming and found I liked it. I enjoyed not having to stare at a black line on the bottom of the pool, and I wasn't a slave to pool time. So for fun I entered a local 10K in Battle Creek, Michigan, and I won. I thought, That was easy, not realizing I was in good shape because I was a swimmer, plus I had youth on my side.

My freshman year at Michigan I qualified for the Olympic Trials in swimming but the U.S. boycotted the 1980 Games and the swimming trials were canceled, so I took the summer off and went to Wyoming. While there, I started running to stay fit, and when I returned for my sophomore year at Michigan I gave up a full scholarship in swimming and joined the track team as a walk-on. I can tell you there were tears in my dad's eyes when I finally got up enough nerve to tell him I had quit swimming to join the cross-country team. He didn't even know what cross-country was; he just didn't get it. After seeing my first cross-country meet he described it to my mom by saying, "They run off into the woods, disappear for twenty minutes, and then come back and finish."

In 1984, the only Olympic options for woman athletes in distance events were the marathon and the 3000. The 3000 is not even two miles, and I'm a slow white girl. I have no fast twitch muscles whatsoever. Fortunately I chose the marathon, because I went on to have a pretty decent career. I was twenty-two and I went to the 1984 Olympics Trials with nothing in my head other than to do my best, enjoy it, get through it, and be competitive. I finished fourth. Only the top three make the Olympic team. At that time I was really excited. Here I was, fresh out of college, and I finished fourth in the country. That was pretty darn good. I kept running, and the next year I won the Boston Marathon.

In 1988, I went to the Olympic Trials and placed fourth again. I ran my best time. What can I say? It was hilly and I ran the fastest time of my career, but I still finished fourth. I was pretty disappointed. I wouldn't use the word *devastated,* because I was still young, and I had another chance to make the team in the first women's 10,000 meters. With a lap to go I was in third place, and then I was outkicked by Lynn Jennings. I ended up finishing fifth in the 10,000, missing the team by seconds. There again I ran my PR, one of the top ten times in the country, and I was pretty excited. That fall I won the Chicago Marathon and ended up being ranked fourth in the world, but I still wasn't on the Olympic team.

In 1989, I won Chicago again and ran a 2:28. Going into 1992, I thought things would be different and I would finally make the team. However, at the end of 1991, I had a foot injury. I took the month of November off, thinking it would heal and then I could start my training, since the Olympic Trials were in May and by then I'd be good to go. Unfortunately, in the middle of November they announced that the Trials were going to be held in January. All of a sudden I had gone from taking the whole month of November off to having the Olympic Trials in January. I thought, Oh, great. I had to do a crash course in getting fit. I was in good shape, but I had lost three months of training, and once again I finished fourth. This time I was devastated because I didn't do anything wrong. I did everything right until someone changed the Trials date, which directly affected my training and my preparedness. I was a little bitter after that, because I felt the women's committee wasn't taking all things into consideration when they moved the date.

By 1996, when I went to the Trials for a fourth time, I was definitely past my prime. I finished nineteenth. It wasn't meant to be. I had to put the idea of competing in the Olympic Marathon to bed and move on.

How did I repeatedly come back from disappointment? Why did I never give up? I love to compete and I love to run, but if I had boiled all of my self-worth and my entire athletic career down to one race, I couldn't have dealt with it. You can't maneuver and motivate yourself to get out there and do it again if you focus on one devastating race. So instead I focused on my own personal goals. I had my short-term goals and long-term goals. I even had location goals, such as running the Honolulu Marathon. What could be better than running a marathon in Hawaii in December?

Because I focused on new goals in my career it softened the blow of not making the Olympic team. I competed overseas in Europe and in Japan, which was exciting for a small-town girl who grew up in Battle Creek, Michigan. I had a career I loved, and I was not going to let the Olympic disappointment take that away from me. Even to this day when they play the national anthem I get all misty-eyed because I wanted so desperately to wear an Olympic uniform. Maybe I'll coach somebody who goes to the Olympics, or maybe I'll have a child who goes to the Olympics, or maybe I'll just be a spectator. But I'm going to get there. ■

"Happiness is derived from achievement, and achievement is derived from overcoming something that at first might have been difficult. Achievement is a valuable thing in our society and teaches you, as an athlete, that you can overcome fears and you can push through things that are uncomfortable."

MICHELE MITCHELL-ROCHA,
diving coach, University of Arizona

"The only person who can stop you from reaching your goals is you."

JACKIE JOYNER-KERSEE,

world record holder in the heptathlon and winner of six Olympic gold medals

NINE

EMBRACE YOUR COMPETITIVE SPIRIT

"I hope to raise my daughter not to be a spectator, not to be on the sideline. I want her to be on the playing field, no matter what it is. I want her to experience the joy of competition and of sport."

LISA RAINSBERGER,
winner of the Boston, Chicago, Montreal, Twin Cities, and Hokkaido marathons

Nancy
LOPEZ

Nancy says winning her first LPGA tournament as a professional was a big thrill because she didn't know if she could win on the LPGA tour. Winning her thirty-fifth tournament was equally thrilling because that qualified her for the LPGA Hall of Fame. It's interesting to note that both her first victory and her thirty-fifth were on the same golf course in Sarasota, Florida.

I almost make myself miserable because I'm so competitive. I've never admitted that to many people. I've always tried to do everything perfectly and I can't. It bothers me, and that's not good. Everything I do—keeping my house clean, picking up, doing things for my kids, making a bed—I always want it to be just right.

I probably have made my kids crazy, because I always tell them do this, do that, not that way, this way, because my mom always told me if I didn't do it right I was wasting my time. It was bred into me: do things right or don't do them at all.

I've certainly gotten better with age, but for most of my young life I always wanted everything perfect, even though I failed many times. ■

"I have a hard time playing a game of cards with my sister and not getting totally pissed off inside if I'm losing. That inner drive is always there to compete and always to win."

SHEILA CORNELL-DOUTY,

softball's 1996 Player of the Year

"My theory is, if it's not worth winning, it's not worth playing. It doesn't matter whether it is cards or Monopoly or fencing or football. If it's not worth winning, it's not worth playing. I compete in everything I do."

KELLY WILLIAMS,

U.S. women's national saber champion

Juli
INKSTER

Juli was the first person, male or female, to win three consecutive U.S. Amateur golf titles (1980–1982). Tiger Woods accomplished the same feat a decade later. Juli was a member of the U.S. Curtis Cup team in 1982 and the World Cup teams in 1980 and 1982. She was a collegiate All-American for four years (1979–1982) at San Jose State University, and she won the 1982 Broderick Award.

I think that sports for girls, even if they don't do anything professionally, teaches responsibility, leadership, and confidence. In this day and age, you have to have confidence in yourself to achieve anything. I always try to tell my own kids and others that you've got to be a leader. You better be in charge of your life and not have someone else telling you, "This is what you should do." I think that's very important. My parents always gave me the opportunity, but they said, "If you want it, you need to go get it yourself."

I think competing is more important than winning. There have been a lot of times when I've teed it up and I didn't win but I felt like I competed. I felt like this was not my day, but I never gave up, and I tried on every shot, and then next week I'd go get them.

You have to learn how to lose in order to win. What I'm saying is you've got to learn from your mistakes. You've got to learn how to say, "Great shot. You were the better player this week, but next week I'm going to get you." I always try to say nice shot or nice putt, no matter what, and hope my competitors will reciprocate because I think that's the way golf was meant to be played.

The hardest part is when I'm out of contention on Sunday. I always look in the paper if I'm out of it. I always look to see what I need to shoot to finish in the top ten, and that's my goal. So, maybe I'm not winning that week, but if I go from thirtieth place to ninth I feel I've accomplished something. You have to take the little steps before you can take big ones. ■

"I'm mostly competitive within myself. It's not always a matter of having to beat everyone in sight."

SONDRA VAN ERT,
Olympic snowboarder

Debi
THOMAS

Growing up, Debi's figure skating idol was Mr. Frick of "Frick and Frack." They were once the leading comedy team on ice and skated with all the top shows. Mr. Frick is Swiss, and he attended the 1986 World Championships in Geneva when Debi won. That night they danced at the competitors' party, and he performed all his funny moves. "It was the neatest thing," Debi says. "Believe it or not, that's my best memory from Worlds, dancing with Mr. Frick."

My biggest thrill was winning my first National Championship, mainly because the odds were against me. Many people thought that because I was going to Stanford University full time, it wouldn't be possible for me to skate to that level. I wasn't skating well at practices either, which isn't unusual for me. I actually tend to get worried when I'm skating well at practices.

I had won the compulsory figures and I skated a strong short program, but Caryn Kadavy won the short program so there was no way for me to win the competition without winning the free skating program. At first I thought, Oh, boy, this is going to be rough, and then I spent the entire day doing nothing but pacing back and forth in my room convincing myself that I could do it. I was saying, "You can do this, you can do this, you can do this; you can do all these jumps; you just haven't done them all in one program, but you can do all of them." I did a lot of visualization, and that was the turning point for me as far as realizing the importance of the psychology of performing.

I went out for warm-ups and immediately fell three times on my triple loop. I could not land the thing. "You're going to have to take that out of the program," my coach told me. But I said, "I can't. I need it to win." When they announced my name, there was a huge roar. I don't know how I developed this following, but the crowd was really with me.

So I said to myself, "You know what? They want me to win this thing, so let's do it." I just took every element one at a time, and as I landed each one I got more and more excited. When I got to the triple loop it was, like, Here goes nothing. I landed the thing and my mouth dropped. It was an incredible moment. I have never had a crowd or a performance so uplifting. It was just fantastic. It was as though I was bigger than I really was. I had basically overcome poor training leading up to the Nationals because I was trying to be a college freshman and I didn't know my head from my rear end. I was doing all those things everybody said were impossible. I was determined to prove to them that, yes, I *can* go to college and, yes, I *can* become national champion and, yes, I *can* become world champion.

I realized it's 95 percent psychological. You have to train, that's part of it, but you cannot train, and train, and train, and expect your body to go out and do it automatically. That was the one time I really had to pull it from my gut. That's when I realized you *can* do it. ■

"When I was skating well I had fire.
When I wasn't skating well it was
just smoke."

DEBI THOMAS

"On the water I'm very aggressive.
I go for it. I don't hold back. I'm
not afraid of crashing. I'm very
focused. But off the water I am
very easygoing."

KELLY MOORE,
champion windsurfer

"You've got to look for tough
competition. You've got to want to
beat the best."

GRETE WAITZ,
*winner of a record nine
New York City Marathons*

Carol
HEISS
JENKINS

Carol, 1960 figure skating gold medalist, still has further Olympic goals. Her most immediate is to have one of her students on the Olympic team. Carol realizes that becoming an Olympic champion requires a combination of talent, luck, timing, age, and health. She hopes one of her students finds that combination before she retires.

I started skating when I was four years old. The only thing I can remember is skating on the pond and having a wonderful sense of freedom. I still have that same sense of freedom when I'm on the ice. I lace up my skates to coach and I'm in my own little world. I just love it. It's mine. I enjoy it. I'm very competitive as a coach. I just focus in on the lessons. I love it when the kids are so competitive they are just not going to quit on something, and when they finally get it, it's high fives all around. We feel like we've won an Olympic gold medal. ∎

"You just skate for yourself, no matter who is competing. It's just you and the ice."

MICHELLE KWAN,

U.S. national champion figure skater

"When I look back at the Winter Olympics, everything was perfect except for one thing. There are so many great memories. I skated my best and that wasn't good enough, but that's what competition is all about."

MICHELLE KWAN,

Olympic silver medalist in figure skating

Inger MILLER

Inger is the world champion in the 200-meter and her godfather is former sprint great Don Quarrie. Inger started running during her sophomore year in high school and finished third in the 200-meter at the California High School State Meet. By the time Inger was a senior, she was the number two high school sprinter in the nation in the 100- and 200-meter events.

The race starts before you get to the blocks, when your mind is clear. You're just ready to put everything together. You've done the work to prepare and now you're ready to let it all hang out. You have to focus on what it is you are going to do. You visualize what the race is going to look like, where you're going to be at 50 meters and 100 meters, what your arms will look like, what your legs will look like. You visualize how you're going to feel and how you're going to breathe. You're to the point where you don't hear the crowd, you don't hear any of the noise, you don't even hear them announcing you. You are completely focused on your lane and your lane only. The blinders are on.

When I race, it's all about me. It's not about the competition. When I race I can't be worried about who's on my left or who's on my right. What matters is how I'm going to perform. This is true in whatever you do. If you're going to play an instrument, it's about you. It's not about anyone else telling you how to play. Once you've learned how, it's up to you to put it together. ■

"When I'm driving my car, I always want to be the first one taking off at the green light."

INGER MILLER

"I was a tomboy growing up. I beat the boys on my block and climbed trees and we had speed races. I've always been competitive."

INGER MILLER

Amy
VAN DYKEN

Amy won three gold medals in the 1998 World Swimming Championship, to go with her four Olympic gold medals. Amy says she actually enjoys failing because she learns so much more about herself as a person and as a competitor. "Losing is a learning experience that helps you to grow as a person," she says. "When you fail you know what it's like to be second or third. So when you're on the award podium and you're first, you have more empathy for your competitors and you treat them a little nicer."

I'm a very tough competitor. I love the game, but I'm out for blood. I'm out to win and I will do anything that it takes to win. A lot of people have said that some of the things I do aren't sportsmanlike, because I jump up and down and I spit pool water out of my mouth. What I say is if you think that's unsportsmanlike, that's fine, because then you're thinking about me and not thinking about winning. I'm out there to win. There's not one person who goes to the Olympics saying, "Oh, I want to get last place." Everyone wants to win. To me there's nothing more sportsmanlike than bringing a gold medal home to your country.

My greatest victory was winning the 100-meter butterfly in the Atlanta Olympics, which I wasn't expected to win. I remember swimming in my Olympic heat of the 100-fly and touching the wall. I didn't think I had made the finals, and then I saw I had the second best time in the field. My coach, Jonty Skinner, and I immediately reviewed the films and talked to some other coaches, and everyone seemed to think I could win. I couldn't believe these people were talking this way because this wasn't my race. I wasn't even supposed to make the Olympic team in the 100-fly, let alone get in the finals, and I definitely wasn't supposed to win.

So I went into the race thinking, My coach thinks I can win, and I know I've trained really hard, so let's just see what happens. I remember when I got to the halfway point I turned and looked and I was in about fourth place and I got pretty excited because I only had to move up one more spot and I would get an Olympic medal. I hit the 75-meter mark; that's usually when you start dropping your hips and your stroke falls apart. You get really tired, and basically you pretty much look like a drowning fish.

But something happened. I remember closing my eyes, and I just thought of all the hours in the pool I had put in and all the hours in the weight room and the fact that my coach thought I could do it, and all I could think of was, Go, go, go.

I remember hitting the wall, and I turned around and saw my time. It was 59.1. I was thinking, Oh, my gosh, there's no way I don't get a medal, and then they announced over the loudspeaker, "Amy Van Dyken from the United States of America has won the gold medal." I just freaked out. I mean, it was the weirdest feeling in the world, because here I was, I wasn't even supposed to make the Olympic team in this event, and I had won my first individual gold medal. ■

"Winning—it's better than breathing."

AMY VAN DYKEN,

who suffers from asthma

"When Jimmy Connors was young, if I had a shot I could hit down his throat, I did. And then I'd say, 'See, Jimmy, even your mother will do that to you.' "

GLORIA THOMPSON CONNORS,

tennis professional and mother of Jimmy Connors

"I came out here to beat everybody in sight, and that's what I'm going to do."

BABE DIDRIKSON ZAHARIAS,

in L.A. for the 1932 Olympic Games

"You're always, basically, competing against yourself. You expect certain things of yourself, and you're always working toward that personal achievement that makes you feel good."

LEONORE MCDANIELS,
world record pole vaulter
for seventy-year-olds

"Horseshoe pitching is a mind game. Some people pitch fast, some pitch slow. If they know pitching slow bothers you, they'll take more time. They'll get up there and swing and swing and swing. Or, after you get a rhythm, like when you're switching places and they're walking back, they'll walk in front of you, just to get you thinking about them. If you're going to win, you have to keep your mind clear."

BECKY KEMPER,
world champion,
women's horseshoe pitching

"After the Olympics, I participated in several dual meets between the United States and France. One cold morning in the countryside south of Nantes, I was in for a surprise. After a couple of high jumps on the improvised track, I realized the landing pit wasn't grass, it was manure."

ALICE COACHMAN DAVIS,

first African American to win an Olympic gold medal (high jump in the 1948 London Games)

Amy
VAN DYKEN

Amy is an Olympic gold medal swimmer whose aspiration is to work with hearing-impaired children. Amy did not know she had made U.S. Olympic history when she won her fourth gold medal in the 1996 Atlanta Games. It was during the press interview, when she was asked how she felt about being the first American woman to win four gold medals in one Olympics, that she realized what she had accomplished. Amy looked at her coach, Jonty Skinner, who replied, "Oops, sorry, I forgot to tell you. I didn't want you thinking about making history."

I love swimming. It's my life. It's my job. I would much rather be in a pool and a weight room for eight hours a day than sitting behind a desk. That's just my own personal choice. A lot of people think I'm crazy, but I love it.

I love the feeling of waking every morning and knowing I get to do something that's going to improve myself. Every day is completely different. I never have a day that's like the day before, because I keep pushing. I'm learning new things about myself, and I absolutely love stretching my body to the limit and seeing how far I can take it before it breaks.

I don't just sit there and go back and forth and back

and forth. I'm training. With every stroke I take I'm working on some technique I need to practice, like my hand position. A lot of people think you swim with your hands closed and cupped, but that's not the way it is at all. You've got to work on spreading your hands out so the water goes in between your fingers and makes a kind of web.

That's one of the things I work on daily. There are other little things, like rotating your hips at the right point, having your breathing the right way, raising your arms above the water a certain way. When they're below the water they're doing a different thing. With every single stroke, there's a lot to think about. You can actually finish the entire workout without even realizing it. ∎

Chris EVERT

Chris won at least one Grand Slam tennis championship per year for thirteen years. The daughter of tennis pro Jimmie Evert, she had an impressive amateur career that included a winning streak of forty-six consecutive matches. Chris turned pro on her eighteenth birthday, December 21, 1972, and won her first Grand Slam title, the French Open, a year and a half later, in 1974.

There are a lot of people who would just love to win. But they don't know how. In the beginning when I started playing junior tennis, I lost all the time; it wasn't like I was always a winner. My dad put me in tournaments when I was eight, nine, and ten, and I'd lose. I think a lot of it was just being shy, or trying too hard to please my parents. There were a lot of psychological reasons in the beginning.

Then I started to win a few tournaments, and then I won a few more. The more I won, the more I got used to winning. It became routine. It was ordinary for me to win. It was not abnormal. A lot of people get so thrilled when they have a win. They think, Oh, my God, I can't believe I won the match! Well, it's not normal for them.

Winning is a habit, and after a while I liked the feeling it brought me. Not the money, because there was no money in those days. It was more a sense of achieving something, of having a goal. Self-satisfaction, pride: I liked those feelings and I built on them. I think most of my career success was based on *desire*. ■

"I've always felt a champion should never let things like questionable line calls bother her."

CHRIS EVERT

"We play with an absolute will to win. That's what separates us from everyone else."

CARLA OVERBECK,
cocaptain, U.S national soccer team

Julie FOUDY

Julie graduated from Stanford University in 1993. While studying abroad in Spain, she wanted to continue practicing soccer because she was still playing for the U.S. national team. The only practice she could get was playing pickup games with Spanish men. Their reaction bordered on funny. The game would just stop and they'd say, "Where are you from? You're obviously not from Spain. How the heck did you learn to play like that? You're a girl!"

The whole team concept is such a joy for me. I love our team. We've been together for eleven years as a national team, and we're all like sisters and best friends. That's a huge part of why I play. The other part is I'm an extremely competitive person with a lot of energy.

In international soccer, every time you step on the field you're pushed to your limit, playing against the best players in the world. It's always a challenge; and it makes you feel you can reach another level. I love the intensity. I love that you're fighting for your country when you're playing for the United States in the Olympics or in the World Championships. It's a great environment. ■

"I'm so competitive. I play
basketball with my husband.
I get so upset. It's a mental battle.
I lose every time. I can't even talk
to him after the game. I think,
Look, get a grip, woman. Get ahold
of yourself."

JULIE FOUDY

"We're women who like to knock
people's heads off, and then put on a
skirt and go dance."

BRANDI CHASTAIN,
U.S. national soccer team star

JJ ISLER

JJ is one of the top female sailors in the world, and she remembers the Barcelona Olympic ceremony when she received her bronze medal. When the music started, JJ realized she should do exactly what other medal winners had done when she watched them at home on television. JJ now felt she had a link with all of the athletes in every Olympics. That was the high point of her Olympics, and she still gets chills thinking about it.

What I love about my sport is that every time you're out on the water the winds are slightly different, the waves are changing, the current is shifting. While you're racing you must stay as open as you can to all these different inputs. Part of it is staying relaxed so you're aware if, all of a sudden, dark clouds build up in one corner of the horizon, or you notice the water is a different color, or you sail over a line of seaweed, indicating a change in the current. It's a matter of knowing which variable is going to be the dominant one. There are times when you may see a current difference but it really doesn't mean much. The next day, however, it could be the overriding factor.

Mental attitude and visualization are so important. This was what I practiced during the America's Cup. We live about twenty minutes away from Point Loma, and on my drive home every day I would replay the key incidents in the race over and over and run all the different scenarios in my head. This wasn't something I had to force myself to do, it was something I loved.

I found myself drawn to this puzzle. I'd find myself thinking, Okay, I've solved one scenario, but what if my opponent had done this instead, how would I have reacted? I couldn't go to sleep at night until I had run all the different scenarios through my head, all those different situations. You realize you may have lost the race because you didn't tack at your first opportunity; instead, you waited twenty seconds. If you replay it in your head, you can see yourself tacking at the right time as opposed to when you did. There's really such a very small difference.

I'd go to sleep at night having replayed the race, seeing myself do everything right, not making any mistakes, reacting to all the different moves of my opponent, and being successful. So no matter how great a mistake I had made on the racecourse, I'd wake up the next morning having sailed the perfect race so many times in my mind that I was ready to go. ■

Sylvie BERNIER

Sylvie, a Canadian Olympic champion, won the gold medal in springboard diving in 1984 in Los Angeles. She says it's very hard to talk about the feeling that came over her when she was standing on the podium after winning the gold medal and the Canadian national anthem was playing. She thought about all she'd been through: leaving home at seventeen to change cities, coaches, and school and living far away from family and friends. Although difficult, it was worth it.

Once you're at the Olympics, every athlete is almost at the same level, at least the top five in the world are. We're all physically the same, we've trained the same, and obviously we have the talent to be there. I think the difference among the top five in the world is how mentally prepared they are at that time on that day. Mental preparation will make the difference. If the competition were held the next day, the results could be totally different.

Being mentally prepared really affected my results. Instead of being first one time and fifth the next, I was always one, two, or three. That was my main objective my last year. The mental preparation—I call it visualization— was for me a major change in my training program. I would do an hour of visualization every day.

At the beginning I had to go into a room by myself because it was so hard to concentrate. I really had to be alone, with no music and nobody talking. At the end I could do it in a restaurant in the middle of a conversation. I would mentally leave. I would just be gone. In my mind I would be doing my dives. At the end they were absolutely perfect in my head. For me, that was very important, because at the beginning I couldn't even see myself. I was seeing somebody else. When I did see myself I would trip on the board or I would make a big mistake, so I would know there was still a lot of work to do. I would try to see myself do a perfect dive. Once you see yourself do a perfect dive in your head, it's much easier to go on the board and do it perfectly.

A month before the Games I cracked a rib doing some exercises on the floor and could hardly breathe. I went to the hospital, and they told me it couldn't get worse but it was going to hurt very much. I had to drop my training program from 100 percent to 50 percent. I couldn't dive, and the Games were only a month away. I didn't tell anybody. My coach and I went to Phoenix for a training camp, and nobody knew. I was always training on my own. I didn't want anybody to say, "Oh, she's injured," and I didn't want any competitors or anybody else to talk about me. I didn't want to take anything out of my dream. My goal was to win the gold medal at the Olympics; I didn't want anybody to talk about anything other than that. Only my parents and coach knew about my injury; even my friends didn't know. I just wanted to forget it for a month.

I was taking medication to stop the inflammation, but I was very sore and I was so anxious at the beginning. Then

I really started to work on visualization again. Instead of training two or three hours a day, I was doing at least an hour and a half or two of visualization because I couldn't dive. I really believe that saved my career. For many months and years afterward my rib was still sore. But I didn't mind, because I retired a week after the Los Angeles Olympics. ∎

"As long as you have fun, as long as you enjoy it, as long as you work the best you can, do what you want, but don't waste your time."

SYLVIE BERNIER

"I tell young kids to play a lot of tournaments, because you want to learn competition and learn to fight and to concentrate. If you just practice all the time, you don't get competitive. You've got to be very competitive. I call it being tournament tough."

DODO CHENEY,
winner of more than three hundred U.S. national women's tennis titles

"On the ice I'm aggressive. To race is to go all out, every time, no matter what happens. I never worry about falling."

BONNIE BLAIR,
winner of six Olympic gold medals in speed skating

"My position of linebacker is very physical. I slam my body so hard, I get headaches and have bruise-covered arms. You can't tell I'm a girl by the way I play—only by my ponytail. Football doesn't have to do with sex or size. It only has to do with determination. You can't listen to other people; you just have to do what's in your heart."

LISA WELCH,
fifteen-year-old football player from Midland Park, N.J.

Dawn STALEY

A three-time Kodak All-American basketball player at Virginia, Dawn was named USA Basketball and U.S. Olympic Committee Female Athlete of the Year in 1994. After Dawn's outstanding basketball career at the University of Virginia, where her number 24 was retired, the only opportunities available for her to play professionally were overseas. Her travels included Italy, Brazil, Spain, and France. With the emergence of the WNBA, she is thrilled to be back playing in the United States.

I love the spontaneity of basketball. It's a thinking person's game. A lot of people think basketball is complicated. It's really a simple game, but a lot of people make it difficult by trying to do things they don't practice. Part of the game is instinctive, but part of it also is being a student of the game, learning why you make certain moves on a court.

I do a lot of clinics, and what I try to teach is why you do things on the court. Learn from your mistakes. Learn why you should make a bounce pass versus a chest pass. Learn why you should shoot a shot rather than penetrate. Learn how to get to the basket by seeing what your defender does. Many people don't put a lot of thought into basketball when they're playing it.

I pay attention to details. I pay attention to what people are doing. I think that's a lost art. I don't know if it's the commercialism of women's basketball, or if little girls are not seeing the basic fundamentals being played, or if they're not looking for them. I think they're just waiting to make a spectacular play. ∎

"If it's the last shot I want the ball. I don't want it necessarily to score, I want the ball so I can make the right decision, whether to score or whether to dump it off to someone else."

DAWN STALEY

"No matter what a kid does in life, they're going to have to compete for something. They're going to have to compete for a grade, they're going to have to compete for a job, they're going to have to compete for everything they do, both girls and boys. Sports teach you how to compete. How to win and how to lose."

NANCY LIEBERMAN-CLINE,

head coach of the WNBA Detroit Shock

Silken LAUMANN

Silken battled her way back from a terrible rowing accident that happened just ten weeks before the 1992 Barcelona Olympics, and captured the bronze medal in the single sculls. However, her athletic career wasn't over; she still wanted to go for the gold. Four years later in Atlanta she had a great showing on Lake Lanier, winning a silver medal. Although she was disappointed in the result, she was not disappointed in her performance because she had done everything she could. Someone was just better that day.

My original plan was to retire in 1992. I was at the right age, and I had accomplished a lot of things. But after my accident, I felt I really hadn't been able to reach my full potential. I had a desire to continue and aim for the gold medal in 1996. However, I had some interesting and trying experiences over the next four years. First, I took 1993 off. Then in 1994, they changed the starting procedure at the World Championships. They had about seventy-plus false starts but since I double–false started I was eliminated. That whole year of training was gone because of that one mistake. Next, in spring 1994, I had a cold and I took a medication that contained a banned substance. Because of this, my gold medal was taken away in the 1995 Pan America Games. Although I had experienced this series of frustrating and difficult incidents, I went into 1996 feeling really strong, believing that this was as good as I could get. I had reached my potential.

I raced extremely well in Atlanta. My final race was flawless. But there was somebody who was better than I was and that was frustrating. Yekaterina Khodotovich from Belarus was awesome. She just came around at the wrong time for me. In 1995, she was seventh in the world and improving rapidly. Then in 1996 she was incredibly powerful.

It's important to know, though, that at the end of the day it's not the medals you remember. You put them in your drawer somewhere and to a great extent they're forgotten. What you remember is the process—what you learn about yourself by challenging yourself, the experiences you share with other people, the honesty the training demands—those are things nobody can take away from you whether you finish twelfth or you're an Olympic champion. That's the greatest joy in my sport. It builds character. That's what rowing has done for me and this will be the biggest thing I'll take from it.

I left my athletic career feeling very satisfied with what I had done. I read once that the best thing you can say of any career is that you went as far as you could go and have no regrets. I can honestly say that about my rowing career. ∎

TEN

BE A ROLE MODEL

"The term role model is too often applied to people whose accomplishments we admire. They've won a medal or made a million dollars or have become a surgeon. These things are admirable. But true role models are those whose character has set an example."

LIZ DOLAN,
*former Nike corporate executive,
later president of Dolan St. Clair,
sports marketing consultants*

Kerri
STRUG

Kerri won an Olympic gold medal in gymnastics at the 1996 Atlanta Games, despite a badly sprained ankle. She says success is becoming the best you can be personally, but always striving for more. Kerri thinks that setting goals, trying to accomplish them, and never giving up are all a part of success. Another part of success is having a good time. With this in mind, she ran the Houston Marathon and finished in 4:12:06. Kerri's reason for running: "I'm sick of doing serious stuff. I want to do cool stuff."

I love being a role model. It's really great. I really love kids, and I feel I can identify with them. I'm short; I have a high voice. It's like I'm just one of them. It's so much fun. I remember the impact people I looked up to had on me when I was young. It can really make a difference if there's one teacher or one friend or one celebrity you can look up to because it gives you a little more incentive. When you're five, six, or seven years old, it means so much.

To be a role model doesn't require much from me. A little note, a smile, a picture, or giving kids a few encouraging words makes their day. It's human nature to want to please other people and to want people to like you. It just feels really good because I'm making some difference. ∎

"As people teach their children about competition, about the ups and downs and how to deal with them, I guess I can stand as a role model. They can say, 'She didn't win but she's still standing tall and smiling and loving her sport.'"

MICHELLE KWAN,
Olympic silver medalist in figure skating

Katie HNIDA

At Colorado's Chatfield High School, Katie was a football placekicker and homecoming queen—a dual achievement Sports Illustrated called "One of the top ten sports moments of the 90s." Nationwide, according to the National Federation of State High School Associations, Katie is among 779 female football players. This is a figure that is growing every year.

It's neat being a role model for younger girls because I think today's girls especially need women they can look up to. A lot of the time, if they are looking up to women who are called jocks, they think you either have to be a jock *or* you have to be feminine. I'm really a combination of both. I still look like a girl; I'm not some big brute. I've got long hair, I wear make-up, I wear skirts to school, but at the same time I'm ready to go kick butt on the playing field. I don't worry about my hair or anything when I'm in the game, but I like to look nice sometimes. You can be a girl *and* be an athlete. ■

"If I had to pick between being feminine and being a jock, I'd probably go jock all the way."

KATIE HNIDA

"I know I looked gross at Homecoming during halftime. No makeup or anything. But I'm a football player. How else am I going to look?"

KATIE HNIDA

JJ
ISLER

JJ was an original member of the 1995 America's Cup all-women's team. She has a roomful of sailing awards. In addition to her Olympic bronze medal and three World Championships, JJ won more than ten national and European championships. Other victories include the Women's 470 World Championship, the IYRU Women's Double-Handed World Championships, the Rolex International Keelboat Championship, and the One Design 48 Class at Key West. She was selected Rolex Yachtswoman of the Year three times: 1986, 1991, and 1997.

In sailing, most of the top sailors are men—guys like Lowell North, Dennis Conner, and Dave Ullman. Somehow my parents raised me so I still thought of those men as role models. It didn't occur to me that I shouldn't use them as role models because they were the other sex.

Now, as the mother of two daughters, I find myself thinking, How did my parents do that? I hear so many people say it's important for young girls to see me out sailing, so they know they can keep doing it. Does your role model have to be the same sex or the same color as you are? I would hope that people, true leaders, could be more optimistic and see themselves in anyone and get past that superficial thing of what their sex is or what the color of their skin is. Use anyone you want as a role model. ■

"Tamara McKinney, the first American woman ever to win an overall World Cup skiing title, was my hands-on role model. That lasted until I started racing against her. That's when she became a *competitor.* I said, 'You're no longer my role model, my idol. You've taught me everything there is to know. Now it's time to beat you.' "

PICABO STREET,

Olympic gold medalist

Claire
CARVER-
DIAS

Claire is a member of the Canadian synchronized swimming team. Canada is currently in a rebuilding mode to regain its former position as the most powerful country in the world in synchronized swimming. Although relatively new on the world scene, Clair Carver-Diaz could hold the key to Canada's success. She has the potential to be one of the best synchro performers in the world.

We love being role models. Everyone has different personalities, right? I'm the kind of person who loves talking to kids and going to speak at schools. I love the fact that I get to do this today because one of my passions is leading by example and experience. The other girls serve as role models by sharing their expertise and coaching in their spare time to help kids learn technical skills.

We all manifest our talents in different ways. For example, some girls like to hang out with younger kids, and some like doing more formal things. But we all feel that it's our responsibility as young Canadians and national team members to be good examples for the upcoming athletes. They're the future. ■

"If you're looking only to win, you've lost the entire reason for sport."

CLAIRE CARVER-DIAS

Joan BENOIT SAMUELSON

Joan was the winner of the 1985 Sullivan Award, which recognizes the most outstanding amateur athlete in the United States. It is one of the most coveted awards in sports. She believes that athletes who are pushed by parents wanting to live vicariously through them, or by coaches wanting to share the limelight, are the athletes who really fear failure.

I didn't set out to become a role model, but it comes with the territory and a responsibility comes with it as well. I wish more athletes would realize that. How I conduct myself in public when there are youngsters and aspiring athletes around is something I'm very aware of.

We have two young children, and they're now starting to play different sports. I speak out against pushing kids at too young an age into competitive and organized sports, and now I'm finding I have children with the same sports passion my husband and I share. Where do you draw the line between cheering and pushing?

The important thing is children should be introduced to a variety of sports and disciplines. Very few young superstars make it through the ranks, and those who do either go on to have great careers and live happily ever after or have a hard time dealing with their success. They find they're living lives that aren't totally constructive and happy. Some who don't make it even after putting everything into it have a hard time coping afterward.

It's important to develop the passion and the love for sports in a variety of different areas. What you learn from other areas of your life helps you when you decide to focus on one particular sport or discipline. Because you've done other things, you have something to fall back on if that one discipline doesn't pan out. ■

**"Don't aspire to be like me.
Be better. Shoot higher."**

FLORENCE GRIFFITH-
JOYNER,

*winner of three gold medals in track
at the 1988 Seoul Olympics*

Lisa RAINSBERGER

Lisa, a champion swimmer and marathoner, thinks winners are the most optimistic people. "Look at the ones who are winning," she says. "They're thanking someone or just smiling from ear to ear. They're not negative people, but rather self-assured and positive. Winners are people who always think the glass is half full. That's the difference."

I like being a role model. I really do. I'm proud of what I've accomplished. I love interacting with people, and I like the look in little girls' or little boys' eyes when they're asking me for advice or for an autograph. I hope that it doesn't sound too egotistical, but I get really tired of athletes saying they didn't choose to be a role model. They chose to be a great athlete—and along with being a great athlete comes the responsibility of being a role model.

I like it. I'm not going to fight it. There are moments after a race, especially in Japan, when I'm bone tired and all I want to do is go back to the hotel and shower and eat. I'll be standing there in a sea of two hundred people. Do I go back to the hotel and not interact with the crowd, or do I stand there and enjoy it? You can bet I'll send my husband off to get me a cheeseburger while I sign autographs, because I'm not going to miss out on this. ■

"When you play, when you win
the gold medal, you aren't just
playing for yourself, you aren't just
winning the medal for yourself.
You're winning it for thousands of
little girls across the country who
want to do what you're doing."

PATSY MINK,
*U.S. congresswoman from Hawaii and co-
author of Title IX*

Charmaine
HOOPER

Charmaine is an outstanding member of Canada's national soccer team. She attended school at North Carolina State University, where she was a three-time All-American. Professionally, Charmaine played four years in J-League in Japan, where she was twice the league's leading scorer. Returning to North America, she was MVP of the W-League with the Chicago Cobras, and 1999 MVP of the FIFA World All-Star exhibition game against the United States.

You know what the sad thing is? I can't really say I've had any role models. I think it's because I grew up in a time when there were no women in soccer. Now I can definitely say that I'm happy to be a role model for younger players.

My responsibility as a role model is to go out and show these younger players that hard work really brings success. And even though you have success, there isn't any reason why you shouldn't continue to work hard. I try to be myself to these players. Even though I may be more well known or get a lot of publicity, it really doesn't change me as a person or as a player. I'm always the same person, the same player. I try to be open to these youngsters and not feel too important to talk to them or give them a few minutes of my time. If I'm going to sign autographs, I want to talk to the kids and see how they enjoyed the game and chat with them for a little bit. ∎

"You should enjoy what you are doing, and if you enjoy what you are doing you are going to do well, and then you'll get better at it."

CHARMAINE HOOPER

"I love being a role model! To know someone looks up to you and wants to be like you is the most satisfying thing I get out of soccer."

KRISTINE LILLY,
world record holder for most player appearances, male or female, in international soccer

"Most of us didn't have soccer role models growing up. We played because it was fun, and maybe, if we got good, soccer could be a ticket to college. But the Olympics, the World Cup, a professional league: those were dreams you kept to yourself. Now we have a whole generation of girls who could actually become professional soccer players. They're our future, and it's up to us to instill in them the same love of the game we have."

SHANNON MACMILLAN,
star midfielder on the
U.S. women's soccer team

"I want to make a lasting impact in the sport of soccer and take advantage of the great opportunities being an athlete presents: helping kids, teaching the sport, being a positive role model."

MIA HAMM,
considered the world's best all-around
women's soccer player

Chris EVERT

The Women's Sports Foundation named Chris the greatest woman athlete of the last twenty-five years in April 1985. When she was sixteen years old, Chris played Billie Jean King in the semifinals of the U.S. Open tennis championship. As they were walking up to Centre Court, Billie Jean said, "You're riding on the crest of a wave." What Billie Jean was really saying was, "Enjoy it now because it's not going to happen again. Once you've made it, they've never going to be rooting for you the same way anymore."

I think people should look at athletes as role models as far as their dedication, their hard work, their commitment, their mental abilities, and their concentration, but that's it. People should not think of athletes as role models off the court or off the field. Everybody's got skeletons in their closet and everybody's human. I should be a role model for tennis players. But as far as an example of how you should live your life, no way. I've done stupid things. I've made mistakes, everybody has; you just try to be a good person.

I get very nervous when kids look up to athletes. It's great to admire them for how they got there and for being a good sport. But that should really be it. When they're in their arena, they're role models, but outside the arena, it's too much pressure to be a role model. ∎

"There are role models all around. Chris Evert, an unknown sixteen-year-old, got to the semifinals of the U.S. Open. It was the first time I realized a girl could be great. It changed my entire perspective. I thought, Well, wait a minute, maybe I can be a professional athlete. Chris Evert changed my whole life."

MARY CARILLO,
professional tennis player
and television commentator

Dawn STALEY

An outstanding athlete, Dawn has started her own foundation to provide after-school programs for girls. At five feet six inches, Dawn is the shortest player on the U.S. national basketball team. She wears a rubber band on her wrist while she plays and snaps herself every time she commits a turnover. Dawn considers her mother, Estelle Staley, to be the person who has given her the most inspiration.

When I talk to young girls, I tell them the motto I live by, "You have to do what you don't want to do to get what you want." If they look at me as a role model, I tell them everything that went on. I think they choose me as a role model because of my successes. A lot of people notice when you succeed, but they don't see what it takes to get there. So, I tell them a little bit about my life, the way I grew up, what people thought about me, and then I'll ask them if I'm worthy of being their role model.

I like being a role model, but not because of what I've accomplished in basketball. It's because of what I try to do off the court in the community. I started my own foundation called the Dawn Staley Foundation. I try to give back in the same manner that the guys in my neighborhood gave to me. I like things really simple. I like things pure, and that's what they instilled in me. I try to instill that in the girls who participate in my after-school program. Nowadays people make life so complicated. If you keep it simple, you can keep the complexity out of it. I think a lot of people want a lot of things in life, but they don't know how to get them.

You see people driving around in new cars, you see people who have nice big houses, and you want those things. But you don't know how to go about getting them. I tell girls that the best way to get them is not bouncing a basketball. Although you may look at me and see me being very successful playing basketball, basketball isn't the only thing I've done. I've graduated from college. I put that up against any athletic thing I've done; I'll get more out of my degree than I will out of my gold medal. A gold medal was my lifelong dream, but if I hadn't gone to college I wouldn't have had the opportunity to play for the Olympic team. Kids often don't realize how academics and athletics go hand in hand.

We have an athletic hour in our after-school program. I don't even attend it. When I had to fill in for one of the site leaders who wasn't there, one of the girls said, "This is the first day you've ever stayed for the athletic hour." I told her, "I never go to the athletic hour because it's not really important to me; it's your life skills and academics that are important to me."

I use my athletic background to reel them into the program, but when I have them there I want them to see how important it is to learn to read and write and develop life skills rather than just play basketball. I tell them basketball doesn't come as easy to you as it does to me, so you need to concentrate in other areas.

Since the ABL folded, there are now only about 100 women professional basketball players in the United States. I ask kids, "What do you think your chances are in becoming one of them?" I tell them, slim to none. That's a rude awakening for them, but I hope they'll catch on and understand what I'm saying. Their best bet is academics. No one can get cut from an academic All-America team. Your grades speak for themselves. But you can always get cut from an Olympic team—or any other athletic team. ■

"Men will say, 'I want to be Michael Jordan,' but women say, 'I admire the athleticism of Jackie Joyner-Kersee.' They never say they want to *be* that person. And that's great for women. They're not molding themselves after someone they see, they draw from six or seven sources. When they are pushing themselves it's from something they feel inside. Like for me, I'm doing everything that feels natural for me. It's an expression of what I see myself doing."

GABRIELLE REECE,
pro beach volleyball star

Nancy
LOPEZ

Nancy loves to tell about the morning she was in the hotel elevator on her way to a tournament. She was completely decked out with sponsor identification prominently displayed on her visor and on her golf bag. A teenage boy in the elevator got that look of recognition on his face and asked, "Are you Sara Lee?"

I like being a role model because there are so many little kids out there who I hope want to play golf. I want to inspire them, because I think professional athletes should do that. Kids need to have someone they can admire, because there are so many bad things out there trying to drag them in other directions. If sports can keep them out of trouble by giving them a role model they want to follow, I want to be that person.

I have three daughters, and I want to teach them the right way in life. I'm going to teach them what my mom and dad taught me. I hope they will make the right decisions, think twice before they do something that's not right, and then decide not to do it.

I feel that way even more now, because even though I've gotten older and I'm more out of the limelight, more and more kids come up to me. I'm talking about ten- and eleven-year-olds playing golf who look at me and say, "You're my favorite golfer." For them to say that to me means a lot, because I think, How does that child know me? Do their parents talk about me? Do they read about me? For them to say that to me makes me feel I'm accomplishing what I've wanted to do all my life in professional golf. I want to be remembered as one of the best players who ever played golf and as one of the friendliest. ∎

"My role model in golf was JoAnne Carner, whom I always admired because of the way she was on the golf course. No matter how she was playing she never showed her emotions in a bad way."

NANCY LOPEZ

Juli
INKSTER

Juli joined the LPGA tour in 1983 and won her first title in her fifth start. She was named LPGA Rookie of the Year and became the first rookie to win two major championships in one season: the Nabisco Dinah Shore and the du Maurier Ltd. Classic. Juli joined Pat Bradley as the only woman to have won the career Grand Slam in the modern era, and was voted the 1999 Player of the Year by the Golf Writers Association of America.

I don't really consider myself a role model. I've always tried to do what's right and I've tried to treat everybody the same. I really enjoy what I do and I've got a lot of support, so I don't mind being a role model, if that's what I am. I would like my kids to know they can do whatever they want and also have a family and be an accomplished person in any walk of life. If little girls growing up can see that I can do it or see that Nancy Lopez can do it, that's great. For women right now the sky's the limit. I'm glad we're in an era where you can go out and sweat and then put on a dress and go out to dinner.

When I travel it's a zoo. My husband, Brian, is the most supportive person I've ever seen. When I'm gone, he's getting the kids up and ready for school and cooking them dinner, and of course he has a full-time job. But we've done it. We've been married nineteen years and the hardest part is trying to get everyone where they're going. It's tough to arrange the kids' schedules, my schedule, and Brian's schedule and get them to mesh. The other part is pretty easy, especially now that we don't have to travel with the high chairs, the diapers, the port-a-cribs, and the car seats. ■

"I still love it. I still love practicing. I still love golf. If I could just show up on Thursday and tee up, it'd be great. It's the travel and the practice rounds that kind of wear on you."

JULI INKSTER

Layne
BEACHLEY

Layne says her greatest surfing victory was her first victory, in Sydney, Australia, where she grew up. She reached that ultimate goal of proving to her friends, her family, and herself that she could win. "Winning relieves a lot of pressure," Layne says, "because there are always times when you doubt yourself. But then after that first win you wonder, Why on earth did I prevent myself from doing it for so long?"

I know I'm a role model, but sometimes it frustrates me. There are some things I can't say and can't do because people are watching me. Young girls look up to me and say they want to be just like me. If they see me chucking tantrums and throwing my board because I lost, that's bad. So I always watch what I'm doing in public.

I quite enjoy the honor of being a role model because it inspires people, and that's my main goal. If I'm going to be a role model, I want to be an inspirational one. I want to motivate girls even if it's outside of surfing. I want to get them to be excited about doing things, to believe in themselves, to have confidence. It doesn't have to be in sports.

I want them to have confidence in themselves and not let people put them down or make them feel weak or worthless, because the more they put you down, the more you need to get back up and prove how wrong they are. There are so many people out there who will tell you that you can't, and what you've got to do is turn around and say, "I can. Watch me." ∎

"I would like to be remembered as someone who, even through trials and tribulations, can be an inspiration to other people who are also down and out. To give them hope and just be a role model."

JENNIFER CAPRIATI,

brilliant young tennis player,
trying to make a comeback after
a few turbulent years

Nancy LIEBERMAN-CLINE

One of the most famous female basketball players in the United States, Nancy believes there's no substitute for hard work. She says, "If you work hard and you prepare yourself as an athlete and you're in great shape, you might get beat, but you'll never lose. Losing is when you're not prepared. On any given day you'll get beat, because that's just sports."

When I have a chance to interact with kids, I realize it could be the only five or ten seconds they will ever see me, talk to me, or touch me. This moment will be the impression they walk away with for the rest of their lives. It really has made me look in their eyes and smile at them. Now, I'm not in a rush. My autograph is horrible-looking because I scribble it, but I'd rather scribble and look in their eyes and pat them on the head and joke around with them. ∎

"I love being a role model. It's the coolest thing in the world. A lot of athletes complain about it, but with me, what you see is what you get. I don't have to act differently in public than I do in private because I'm just the same. It's the neatest thing in the world to have a conversation with someone who thought I was untouchable. When I sign an autograph for a little kid it's an honor."

AMY VAN DYKEN,
Olympic gold medalist and Women's Sports Foundation Female Athlete of 1996 in swimming

"It doesn't matter what place you get or how much money you make or what kind of car you drive, it's how you feel about yourself and how other people view you. If other people view you as a role model and you know you're the best person you can be, I think you're successful."

AMY VAN DYKEN

Jean
DRISCOLL

Jean is a seven-time winner of the Boston Marathon's women's wheelchair division. She logs 150-mile weeks to prepare for a marathon. Long "runs" are twenty-five miles. Speed work often consists of mile repeats done in three minutes flat. Her aluminum wheelchair weighs seventeen pounds, and she uses special gloves to literally punch the push rims that are connected to the carbon fiber wheels. Jean tips the scales at 112 pounds and bench-presses 210 pounds.

I love being a role model and having the platform. I love making people feel good about themselves, and I love challenging kids to "dream big and work hard." When kids say they want to grow up and win the Boston Marathon, it bothers me that some people say, "Why even try?" Yes, the chance of that happening is next to nothing. But if you are committed enough and make the sacrifices, you can make anything happen.

These days a lot of people feel it's a risk to dream big, and they aren't willing to make the sacrifices to work hard. Too often our biggest limitations are the ones we place on ourselves or the ones we allow others to place on us.

I'd always dreamed about being a good athlete because those were the most popular people in school and they seemed to be the most successful. All of a sudden I have gone beyond my dreams. If someone had told my parents, "One of your five children is going to be a world record holder and an Olympic champion," I would not have been even a part of the equation. For gym class in school I used to go and help the art teacher. (I'm terrible at art.)

I have a very strong Christian faith, and I believe God has been performing miracles throughout all my life. I just never recognized them until the last couple of years when I've been able to look back. I flunked out of school, yet ended up graduating with honors, and now I have a master's degree. I was once seen as somebody who was going to be a secretary because that was a sit down job and something I could do with my hands. Well, I have a sit-down job and I'm doing something with my hands—pushing my racing chair.

And now I'm at the top, at the pinnacle of sports, and I am not just a role model for people with disabilities. People who don't have disabilities look up to me. I've always wanted to fit in and be "normal." The braces made me feel different. The way I walked made me feel different. The wheelchair made me feel different. The inability to have regular control over going to the bathroom *really* made me feel different. Now I know I am indeed different, but in a special way. ■

Liz
DOLAN

Liz defines success as "The satisfaction of spending your hours on things that are valuable. Sometimes it's valuable to your family, other times it might be valuable to a particular business that you are associated with, and sometimes it's valuable to your community or the world."

My biggest hero is Rosa Parks. I admire her because she was able to accomplish something truly important just by the strength of her character. What she did is within the reach of all of us—she didn't need money, or a corporate entity to back her, or a university degree. She simply stood up for what she believed in and, in the process, changed the world. She perfectly fits my definition of success: someone who is able to have an impact on her community by being who she is. ∎

ELEVEN

THERE'S MORE TO LIFE THAN WINNING

"The medals don't mean anything and the glory doesn't last. It's all about your happiness. The rewards are going to come, but the happiness is just loving the sport and having fun performing."

JACKIE JOYNER-KERSEE,

world record holder in the heptathlon and winner of six Olympic gold medals

Aimee
MULLINS

Aimee is a challenged sprinter and long jumper whose legs were amputated below her knees when she was a year old. Aimee has been in the forefront as a role model since she was eleven years old, but interestingly, she doesn't picture herself in that role. Probably because she is so busy getting on with her life.

Going to Atlanta for the Paralympic Games, I was confident I would come home with two gold medals. I was totally psyched. I had never lost in a disabled meet. I won a gold medal in skiing. I was on a championship softball team. Our swim team always won. I always seemed to be on the lucky end of these things. Winning was something I expected of myself, so I went to Atlanta expecting to win.

I found out twenty minutes before my first race, when they posted the heat sheet at the warm-up track, that I was in big trouble. I looked at my competition's times in the 100-meter and they were 12.8, 12.5, and 12.3. My fastest time was 15.7! I got on the bus to go to Olympic Stadium and they were all sitting there staring at me. I was the only woman in the world running on a pair of prosthetic legs. They were looking at this incredible novelty, and I was staring at them in complete shock and disbelief, because what they were missing were arms and hands!

Here was Olympic Stadium—what I'd been training for in every meet. This was what it was supposed to culminate in. It's funny. Somebody asked, "Why didn't you back out? Why didn't you just fake an injury?" It never occurred to me not to go through with it, even though it was going to be a disaster. I didn't know whether to laugh or cry. I had always gone into every event to win, but there was a 100 percent chance that I would *not* win this time.

It really made me think about why we undertake the endeavors we do and why I did it. Is the whole purpose just to go and win? It's really not, not for any athlete. Winning is the icing on the cake, but I reflected on the year and three months of preparation. It's an incredibly short time to get to world-class level. I thought about all the people who jumped on board this crazy train I drummed up, of becoming an Olympic athlete in a year. The fact that when I asked for help I got it from Georgetown. The fact that when I was training out in California, the guy at Circuit City gave me a video camera at a special price—some crazy reduction he made up so I could tape myself while running. The fact that people came out in full force to help me go after my dream. That was what was beautiful.

It was like the revelation I had after the Olympics. Okay, you did it all and you didn't win. In fact, you lost huge, so what was the purpose? All that training—was it worth it? Yes, it was, because I willed my life to go in the direction I wanted it to go. I shaped myself as a person through the people I was working with, people I had met.

I don't know if it was a profound revelation; I wouldn't ever turn down a gold medal. But I do know it made me reevaluate my life. ■

"Perfection isn't winning every time. A lot of different factors go into every race, and you can't control all that. Perfection just means doing as excellent a job as you can on that particular day. The people I admire most aren't necessarily the most wonderful athletes. I admire the ones who keep coming back and doing it, time after time."

AIMEE MULLINS

Aimee holds the below-the-knee amputee world record in the 100-meter and 200-meter races.

Aimee MULLINS

There's this saying that always sticks in my mind: The quest for the Holy Grail was not in the cup but in the journey. That summarizes my experience. Sometimes you're achieving glory in the traditional sense of finishing first. Most times the true win is how you grew as a person and as an athlete.

Inevitably you are going to fall and you are going to fail and you are going to have times when you question why you're doing it. You have to know you're doing it for yourself. You got yourself into this, and you are willing yourself to reach higher. You grow both as a person and as an athlete when your ability increases. Your physical body can only take you so far. It's your emotional body, the confidence that you have about yourself as a person, that takes you to the highest level.

Athletics taught me to reflect on how far I've come as a person. I compare goals I set for myself two years ago with the goals I have now. I'm the true twenty-first century athlete with the literal combination of natural talent and technology that you can see. A year ago there was no market for disabled athletes. I didn't have people beating down my door to offer me a contract, but that's starting to change.

My dream is to see disabled sports mainstreamed. I'd love to see the word *disabled* taken away from the event, because it's truly an accomplishment. It doesn't matter that the athletes don't have legs or that they're racing in wheelchairs. The fact is a male amputee will probably soon break eleven seconds in the 100-meter. The world record is 9.79 and right now the disabled record is 11.3. It's about a second and a half off of the able-bodied world-record time, and this guy is missing two feet. I think it's a shame the American public doesn't know more about the achievements of the world's other great athletes. ∎

"People who say they've done it on their own aren't being too perceptive."

AIMEE MULLINS

Gabrielle REECE

Gabby says the games you will always remember are the ones when both teams were giving 100 percent. It was a question of who is willing to be mentally more patient. You remember those games because they are hard—hard to win and hard to lose. "There were times I played the best I could and I still lost. That was really tough," she says.

I'm a competitor, but I don't have to win at everything. I just want to do the best I can, and sometimes the result is successful. I know some people lose their mind if they don't win. In some ways, I feel philosophical. I ask myself how this whole thing affects me. I'm also very aware that my sports life is short compared to my whole life and it's also a small part of it. I'm a tough competitor, but because sports came later in my life, it's not the only thing. I try to fit everything together. When you do that you end up keeping your perspective. ∎

"If you didn't win or you weren't
even voted All-American, that
doesn't mean you weren't successful.
There are times I've played the
best I could and still been beaten,
but I can be done with it and say it
was a success. When you don't feel
successful is when you go only
halfway and then you relive it over
and over because you know you
didn't do all you could do."

GABRIELLE REECE

Claire
CARVER-
DIAS

Claire is a member of the Canadian national synchronized swimming team. She led Canada in the Synchro World Championships against competition from all the top nations. Claire finished a respectable sixth in solo and teamed with Fanny Letourneau for a strong sixth-place finish in the duet. In the team event, Canada achieved its goal of finishing in the top three with a bronze-medal performance.

My favorite memory is the Pan Am Games. We were swimming second and our greatest competitors, the United States, were swimming fourth. We swam to the best of our abilities at that time, and when we finished we could feel by the reactions of the crowd that it was a great swim. Before our competitors even began, we went into the showers, crying and celebrating the fact that we had such an amazing performance. And that was all before the results came out.

The victory wasn't in winning (which we ended up doing), it was in totally swimming our hearts out and being able to celebrate the fact that we had had our best possible swim and entertained the people watching, regardless of how we placed. ■

"The thrill of victory comes from knowing you have done everything possible to achieve your goal."

NICOLE HAISLETT,
Olympic swimming gold medalist

"I used to be tunnel-visioned, but I have been forced by my experiences to look past the tennis. After my career, it will be humbling to start from the bottom with something new. Just because I was good at tennis doesn't mean I will be successful at something else. It's easy to forget about how many hours and years it took to get so far in tennis."

MONICA SELES,
winner of seven grand slam tennis titles,
stabbed in the back in 1993
at a tournament in Germany

"All you can do is your best. You give it everything you have and whether you make it or not, you've done all you can. If you've done that, there's nothing else you can give and you should be proud of yourself."

JOY FAWCETT,
star player on the U.S. national soccer team

Kelly WILLIAMS

Kelly is the U.S. national saber champion. She realizes that she's never going to fence a perfect bout and that's okay with her. As Kelly says, "Every day we're going to make mistakes, but what matters is how quickly we recover from those mistakes and move on with our lives. To me that's what life is about. We make mistakes, we recover, and we learn so that hopefully, we don't make the same mistakes again."

Often we tie who we are and our acceptance as a person into the result of our athletic competition. I need to realize that who I am as a person is not dependent on whether I win or lose a specific touch or bout. During stretches I'm going to win some, I'm going to lose some, and it's not going to change me, and the people who know me and love me—my family and friends—aren't going to change their perception of me. When I feel that who I am depends on whether I win or lose, I can't do it. I can't compete.

The one thing I try to remember is there's nothing I can do today that is going to make me any more or less acceptable in the eyes of my mom, my family, and my God. If I win, I'm no more acceptable than if I finish dead last.

Sports are very emotional, and the emotion is there because you're putting every ounce of energy you have on the line. So when I was on the strip in the championship bout there was a lot of emotion. I knew I'd worked ten years to get to this point, and with one touch I could watch it shift to someone else.

It would have been so easy to allow the expectations to interfere with what I had to do. That's when you look at what you have to lose and what you have to prove. If I feel like I have to prove myself to you on the strip, I have something to lose and it will make it difficult for me to perform. ■

"In 1998, I thought if I didn't win the gold, I'd be less of a person. But when I went through it I realized that's not what I'm made of. One competition doesn't make me who I am."

MICHELLE KWAN,
Olympic silver medalist in figure skating

"Sportsmanship is not just about being nice, it is much more important than that. It's about realizing that you could not compete without an opponent and that she has the same goals as you."

STEPHANIE DEIBLER,

softball player, Allentown College of St. Francis de Sales

"In the Olympics there is a sense of tremendous camaraderie with your competitors. It is part of what I like to call the shared energy of competition. You're not competing against your comrades, you're articipating with them."

ANDREA MEAD-LAWRENCE,

first American to win two gold medals in alpine skiing, 1952 Oslo Games

Cassie CAMPBELL

Cassie plays for the Canadian national hockey team, and they've had great success. They won the gold medal at the 1995 and 1996 Pacific Rim Championships, the 1996 Three Nations Cup, and the 1994 and 1997 World Championships. In addition, Cassie is the spokesperson for the HIP Program that helps keep young girls from smoking and is also the spokesperson for CHA's Speak Out! Campaign against harassment and abuse.

I think winning is important, but at the same time I think the lessons you learn from losing are more important than the ones you're going to learn from winning. You don't tend to learn a lot about yourself when you win. You tend to learn a lot about yourself when you lose. First, you learn how you handle mistakes. You say, "Okay, how can I go about it differently?" When you're losing, there's a lot of negative stuff going on around you; how do you deal with that? Are you still able to be positive, are you able to stay focused, are you able to go on? I think when you win, you just keep going. You just keep on, the same way as you've always done, because you don't want to change anything. You don't really learn anything. When you lose, you learn a lot more. ■

"Success is setting goals for yourself and achieving them. Never compare your successes with other people's successes because that's not what it should be about. It's about your own goals; writing them down on paper and then achieving them. Don't worry about what everyone else is doing."

CASSIE CAMPBELL

Sheila CORNELL-DOUTY

Sheila is a U.S. Olympic gold medalist in softball. The Women's World Cup had its soccer-mom heroes, but the U.S. Olympic women's softball team can go one better. It has a slugging grandma for a hero. But, admits Sheila, she's not your average grandma. "I did it the easy way," she said. "I have three stepchildren and the youngest just had a baby girl." Sheila doesn't have to worry about raising the child. "As a grandmother," she said, "all I have to do is love her and dote on her."

My first international experience was really wild. We played in the Pan Am Games in Caracas, Venezuela. Honestly, the entire trip from A to Z is still to this day almost unbelievable.

We got to the Pan Am Village and it was only half finished. The buildings were there, but they hadn't put up the beds. We didn't have blinds. There were areas for closets but no doors. You'd see plumbing for sinks, washers, and dryers, but none existed. There were wires everywhere but just one little lightbulb in the ceiling. Yet camping out in those buildings was a ton of fun. It was my first experience in a country that was entirely different from home.

Almost everybody got sick at some point. The food was in an open tent, and just the smell of it was nauseating.

I existed on peanut butter and drumstick ice cream cones. The entire time we were there that was all I ate. One day they ran out of peanut butter and I was like, "Okay, what else can go wrong? How could they possibly run out of peanut butter?"

We took a different bus route to the stadium every day because the driver said they were worried about snipers. One day we were out in the middle of nowhere and a teammate was dying to go to the bathroom. No way would they stop the bus, so we were all trying to find some sort of carton so she could at least have some relief.

To top it all, they picked the two women on our team who had never had a drink in their lives for drug testing. To make it worse, on that particular day they didn't have any water to give them. All they had for them to drink, to help them go to the bathroom, was beer. By the time they came back to the Village they were pretty smashed. That was my first international experience. It was a classic from beginning to end. ■

"Either you have your dreams or you live your dreams. I'm not all that remarkable. I just keep putting one foot in front of the other until I get to where I have to go. Everybody's got their finish line in life. This is mine. People need to know that success isn't all about winning."

ZOE KOPLOWITZ

Suffering from multiple sclerosis, Zoe completed the New York City Marathon in 28 hours. She made the walk to her finish line (26 miles, 385 yards) with the aid of two custom-made canes, where she was greeted by her friend Grete Waitz.

"Do I want to make the Olympics? Yes. Do I expect it? No. You can never expect anything. To a lot of athletes, the Olympics are the be-all and end-all of human existence. But in terms of life, there is just so much more out there."

JENNY LINGAMFELTER, *springboard diver and Olympic hopeful*

"I'll go out and surf huge waves, but I'll also be the only one out there when it's ankle high. The ocean, for me, is a place of solitude and spirituality, of joy and pain, a place where science and mystery converge. I try to understand why things happen the way they do, and even though there are no answers, the process brings me peace."

SARAH GERHARDT, *first woman to surf a wave at Maverick's, the Northern California break regarded by many as the most dangerous on earth*

Jacqueline GAREAU

Rosie Ruiz was the first woman to cross the finish line in the 1980 Boston Marathon. Unfortunately, she neglected to run the first 25 miles of the course, and even more unfortunately, she stole the limelight from Canadian marathoner Jacqueline Gareau, who had run the race in a record time of 2:34:28. The media was immediately suspicious of Ruiz's finish, so they examined 10,000 official race photos and couldn't find her in a single one. A week later, Jacqueline was named the official winner.

When I crossed the finish line I heard cheering, but it wasn't very loud for a winner of the Boston Marathon. I didn't think too much about that, however, because when you finish a 26.2-mile marathon, just finishing exhilarates you.

When I first saw Rosie Ruiz, she was surrounded by interviewers. After questioning her the reporters came to me, all with the same question: "Did you see her?" "No," I answered.

I met Rosie in Miami at an Orange Bowl 10K a couple of years later. She approached me and introduced herself. I asked her, "Why did you do that?" She answered, "I did run it, and I will do it again." I just turned around and started talking with someone else.

As I look back, I have no feeling of animosity toward Rosie. I have more of a feeling of fondness for her, because I think deep inside she probably doesn't feel all that good about herself. ■

"Winning is always a good possibility. You never exclude that. But it is not really a must. The must is to achieve your potential, what you trained for."

JACQUELINE GAREAU

"I'm forty-six years old and I still race. I stay in shape, and once in a while I surprise myself."

JACQUELINE GAREAU

Sylvie BERNIER

Sylvie, who won the Olympic gold medal in springboard diving in 1984, is also a television star in Canada. She hosts a weekly health and activity feature on the morning show Salut, Bonjour *for the TVA Network. Then, in the fall, she cohosts the exciting physical and mental one-hour game show* Fort Boyard, *shot on location in France. In addition, Sylvie has also been a television analyst for four Olympic Games.*

I think that deep inside I'm not a competitor against everybody else. I'm not the kind of person who wants to defeat somebody. I don't like that feeling. I remember when I was younger I didn't want to win over my friends. I wanted to do well, but at the same time if I could be second and do well, I was happy. I had to change that feeling over the years and say, "Okay, I'll stop looking at everybody else and saying, Wow they're incredible, and say, Okay, I'm here because I'm as good as they are."

Now I know that, so I stop losing my energy on everyone else. I just concentrate on me and on my training and on the fact that if I do the dives the way I know I can do them, I can win. If I don't win, it's okay. If I don't win and I'm proud of what I've done, then it's fine. I'll just go back home and work on my dives and on what I have to do. That's what I had to learn, and that's why I stopped watching the scoreboard during competition. I just wanted to concentrate on one dive at a time, and it worked for me.

I really tried not to worry about the psychological war, if you can call it that, and I tried to put everything on the side and stress the fact that I was there to have fun. I've done the work I have to do. I'm the kind of person who works very hard, and when I took the airplane to the Olympics in Los Angeles I knew there was nothing more I could do. ■

"Winning a gold medal shouldn't be an aim in itself. I'm proud of my gold medal, but I'm mostly proud of the road I took to get there."

SYLVIE BERNIER

Bonnie
BLAIR

Speed skater Bonnie Blair is the winningest U.S. athlete in Olympic Winter Games history, with six medals, five of them gold. She believes in setting a series of little goals along the way to her main goal. "Go ahead and set those long-range goals," she says. "But if you don't think about the little goals that are going to help you get there, then you're going to make that road a lot longer."

One of the things I focus on most is achieving a personal best. I think, a lot of times in America, people get carried away with winning gold, silver, or bronze, whereas winning doesn't necessarily mean being first in my book.

For instance, in the 1994 Lillehammer Olympics, I was able to come away with two more gold medals, but my best race came in the 1500-meter. I skated that race faster than I ever had in my entire life by half a second, and I finished fourth. I just missed a bronze medal by three-one hundredths of a second, that's how close it was. But the thing is, it was a personal best at that distance. It was actually the first personal best I had achieved in any race since the 1988 Olympics, six years earlier. A lot of people looked at my finish as a disappointment, but to me it was a great highlight.

It's great to win, and I'm not taking anything away from winning, but for me, winning doesn't always mean being first. Winning means I'm doing better than I've ever done before. ■

"Soccer is a game we play, and we are good at, and we spend a lot of time trying to be the best. But it is not who we are, and I think seeing that makes a big difference."

MICHELLE AKERS,
Olympic and World Cup soccer star

"I think success is how you conduct your life, not just if you win games. I want to be great at what I do, but I care how I do it. I don't want to cheat somebody for a win. I don't want to lie to somebody for a job. Success to me is how you handle yourself day in and day out. Success is consistency."

NANCY LIEBERMAN-CLINE,
head coach of the WNBA Detroit Shock

Michele
MITCHELL-ROCHA

Michele was a two-time Olympic silver medalist in platform diving before becoming the coach of the University of Arizona diving team. The highlight of Michele's diving career took place at the World Championships in Shanghai, China, in 1985. Local favorite Zhu Ji Hong, who had defeated Michele in the '84 Olympics, had just drilled her final dive. Then as Michele walked to the end of the platform 33 feet above the water, the twenty thousand Chinese in the stands started tinkling their teacups to distract her. They shouldn't have done that. Michele got really mad—so mad that she hit a perfect dive and won the World Championships.

I don't think kids these days, whether they're in college or high school, have enough people telling them they love them for themselves. I think coaches get too wrapped up enjoying athletes because of their abilities. So one of the things I always do is remind our team that I'm committed to them, I love them, and I'll continue to love them. I love them going into the competition, and I'm going to love them coming out of the competition. That love is unconditional, so therefore there is no failure.

My philosophy has always been, and will continue to be, that ten years from now you're not going to remember where you placed in a competition, but you're going to remember the friends you made along the way. You're going to remember the funny days, like the time we were diving in the snow. That's right, we're in Arizona, and we were diving in the snow. No one remembers the workouts when it was 100 degrees, but they'll remember diving in snow flurries. They said, "We're not diving today?" And I said, "Oh, yes, we *are,* and this is going to be one of those memorable days you'll carry in your head forever." To this day, they still talk about how they dived in the snow in Arizona.

Playing sports gives you the opportunity to create these wonderful memories. I don't remember where I placed in the Pac-10 Championships fifteen years ago, but I do remember my teammates and the friendships I made with them. I don't look back and go through my medal collection to figure out what a star I was, but I do pick up the phone and call my teammates and ask them how their children are.

It's all about experiences and relationships, and I really put very little emphasis on winning. The girls do that, I don't need to. I need to keep them relaxed because everyone wants to win. (If you didn't want to win, you wouldn't be in athletics.) But I think somebody needs to point out it's okay to be happy to be a participant too. And that's what I try to do with my girls.

I find that, as my girls graduate, they continue to come back, because the withdrawal is not from the competition, the withdrawal is from being a part of the team. The void in their life isn't necessarily the competitive void. The void in their life is from not being a part of the group dynamic. ■

"I have to remind myself that even
if I have a bad race, it's not the end
of the world, and it doesn't reflect
badly on me, personally. It might
reflect on how I handled that
particular race, but not on who
I am as a person."

HILLARY LINDH,

*downhill skier, world champion, and
silver medalist at the 1992 Winter Olympics*

Debi
THOMAS

Debi was the first African American woman in figure skating to win a gold medal in the World Championships and the first African American figure skater ever to win an Olympic medal. Her most recent major accomplishment was completing her medical degree. Being Debi Thomas, M.D., has been her dream since she was five years old.

A winner is someone who real-izes what her potential is and strives to reach it every time she performs. Sometimes you don't always achieve your potential, but a winner can accept that and learn from it.

I think you don't have to be number one to be a win-ner. There's something called sportsmanship, and there are people who are outstanding athletes whom I don't consider winners because of their attitude and the way they act. Being a winner is going out and doing everything you can to do your best, but also being gracious when you come out on top and gracious when you don't. I know that's a long definition but it's all attitude.

I tell young girls who aspire to be Olympians to make sure they are doing it because they enjoy doing it and not just to win a gold medal. Regardless of the sport they're in, I always advise them not to do it if they think an Olympic gold medal is going to make them rich. I tell them, do it because you love it and because you want to be your best. You have to go out there and do your best, and you can't be disappointed if you don't get a gold medal. You have to be satisfied and proud of your effort.

Unfortunately, our society puts a premium on being number one. These young kids think once they win the gold medal that's the end. They don't realize there is so much more to life. I don't want to see any young girls or young boys not reach their full potential because they didn't get a gold medal.

There are a lot of people who miss out on what they could have been because they focus so much on just getting the gold medal. And then if they don't get it they go into a downward spiral. They never go to college, they don't know how to do anything, they don't have any skills. My advice is that going to the Olympics and winning a gold medal are great goals, and I certainly would never tell anybody to give them up. But the real goal should be to be the best that you can be. ■

INDEX